THE BACK HOME SERIES

SERIES TITLES

PRAISE FOR

THE PAST TEN

"Wow. The 71 essays in *The Past Ten* may be 'fun-sized' (1,000 words max) but boy, do they pack a wallop. While diverse in subject matter, style, settings, and themes, they are all simultaneously heartbreaking and heartmending, even the most harrowing of them full of hope. As co-editor Donald Quist says in his moving Preface, 'I wanted these narratives to inspire others to think about their own existence, and how they have changed over the past ten years, so that they might be encouraged to see another decade.' Mission accomplished—and then some!"

—DAVID JAUSS
author of *Glossolalia: New & Selected Stories*

"What a powerful and brimming treasure trove of stories this is: stories of transformation, of metamorphosis, of loss, of love, and of becoming. And what a persuasive and ingenious ode to time: its waves and meanders, its sharp curves and gentle arms. This book changed my perception of years, and made me desperate for the gift of many more."

—ROBIN MARIE MACARTHUR
author of *Half Wild*

"The essays in *The Past Ten* are full of intimacy and vulnerability, discovery and transformation. A reflective mosaic, made up of some of the most exciting voices in American literature today."

—JAQUIRA DÍAZ
author of *Ordinary Girls*

"Why do we die? Aquinas, working that question, landed on this: Without death life has no meaning. Without that final final, living would be just a bunch of stuff that merely happened. Hence, the genius of the essays collected in *The Past Ten*. The many memoirists assembled here create compelling codas, artificial endings, closing parentheses in order to look back and look closely, sift and sort, assess and assay with gifted elan and elegant exegesis, and see for the very first time these very mean and memorable meanings. The editors of *The Past Ten* have constructed this Thomistic time machine, a server farm of sorts, of meanings, overlayed on the mere stuff that happens, that emerges sublimely from these emergency attempts. Here we can, as we reconnoiter our pasts, imagine our many deaths while we reimagine the one true life we've lived."

—MICHAEL MARTONE
author of *Plain Air: Sketches from Winesburg, Indiana*

THE PAST TEN

an anthology

Edited by
Donald Quist,
Kali White VanBaale,
& Bailey Gaylin Moore

CORNERSTONE PRESS
UNIVERSITY OF WISCONSIN-STEVENS POINT

Cornerstone Press, Stevens Point, Wisconsin 54481
Copyright © 2025 Donald Quist, Kali White VanBaale, & Bailey Gaylin Moore
www.uwsp.edu/cornerstone

Printed in the United States of America by
Point Print and Design Studio, Stevens Point, Wisconsin

Library of Congress Control Number: 2025931785
ISBN: 978-1-960329-75-2

Artwork by Bailey Gaylin Moore.

This is a work of nonfiction. All of the events in this book are true to the best of
the authors' memories. Some names and identifying features have been changed to
protect the identity of certain parties. The authors and editors in no way represent
any company, corporation, or brand, mentioned herein. The views expressed in this
book are solely those of the authors and editors.

Cornerstone Press titles are produced in courses and internships offered by the
Department of English at the University of Wisconsin–Stevens Point.

DIRECTOR & PUBLISHER
Dr. Ross K. Tangedal

EXECUTIVE EDITORS
Jeff Snowbarger, Freesia McKee

EDITORIAL DIRECTOR
Brett Hill

SENIOR EDITOR
Ellie Atkinson

PRESS STAFF
Paige Biever, Sophie McPherson, Kylie Newton, Madison Schultz, Ava Willett

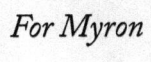

For Myron

PREFACE

Where were you on this day ten years ago?

This question saved my life. Seriously, that is not hyperbole. In 2016, my depression deepened in a way I had never known. The sudden waves of self-hatred and doubt left me drowning in my daily life. I sank to thoughts about how I didn't deserve to live, and how I hadn't done enough to justify my existence. This created a strain on my marriage at the time; my wife didn't know how to help me. She couldn't say enough or do enough, to try to convince me of my value. Nothing could show me my life had worth. I drifted further into a still and quiet void. I formed fissures between myself and loved ones.

My thoughts of suicide became plans. I drafted goodbye letters on my laptop, left passwords and instructions for those to find when I had gone. Outside of my immediate circle of friends, most people could not see the trench I'd dropped into. Professionally, I'd published a successful book with a reputable small publisher. I had a full-time position at a university in Bangkok, Thailand. And, after a lifetime of obesity, I had lost over one-hundred pounds through diet and exercise.

But an emptiness still pressed down on me.

Then one evening I chatted with an older friend who had learned to swim up from a similar chronic blues. He told me about where he was at my age. He spoke to me about how, on that very day years earlier, he could never have imagined how much his life would improve. He couldn't have imagined his overall wellness. Talking to him reminded me that to live is to surf against a wild tide, diving again and again into uncharted instances both familiar and uniquely new. Like many, I'm often guilty of obsessing about the present and forgetting that change is the only promise. Nothing lasts forever, sure, but that means there are infinite chances to find and make new versions of ourselves. Listening to my friend map his journey, I considered where I was at earlier points in my own life. In my mind, I went back a year, then five years, and then ten. I recollected emotions and senses. I reflected on who I was, who I'd become, and how the ocean of time between these selves might reveal who I could be. The question of who I was ten years ago led me to think about progress and encouraged me to float on, if only for the simple fact that *now* would someday turn into a *then*.

I started asking others about their own voyage over the last decade. I found it interesting how everyone approaches the question differently. Each time I'd get an answer that helped me see my own life more clearly. I began reaching out to people who lived farther away, asking them for a brief recollection in writing about where they were on that date ten years ago. I'd ask them to be as specific as possible. I encouraged them to fish through the sights, sounds, tastes, and smells of that day.

Most agreed. They became researchers of their own lives. They scanned through old social media posts, searched through photos, and sorted through letters. I began keeping a blog to keep all the reflections I was getting in one place. Soon I noticed trends between these stories. There was an underlying hope, reminders that change can bring ruin but also rescue. With their permission, I asked to share some of these responses as a way to celebrate the transformative power of time and the magic of humanity to turn the unpredictable into art. I wanted these narratives to inspire others to think about their own existence, and how they have changed over the past ten years so that they might be encouraged to see another decade.

I launched past-ten.com in January 2017. In those early months, I still struggled to paddle out from under waves of depression. I moved back to the U.S., became a full-time care-giver for my mother, survived a failed suicide attempt, gained

seventy pounds, developed a brief dependency on pain medication, and my marriage ended in divorce. Through it all, my
commitment to receiving, reading, and publishing the variety of
recollections for *Past Ten* buoyed me. This project would teach
me to signal for help from others and reach further.

IN 2019, STRUGGLING THROUGH the first year of a PhD program in Creative Writing, familial obligations, and financial
woes, I desperately needed aid to keep up with *Past Ten* and
its growth. Bailey Gaylin Moore, my girlfriend at the time and
now my spouse, stepped in as an editor for the website. She
steadily took on greater responsibilities—soliciting authors,
editing and publishing posts, creating/designing visuals and art
to accompany and promote the texts, and running the social
media accounts. She is now the Editor-in-Chief of past-ten.
com. The project has become as much of a reflection of her
vision as it is mine. There is no timeline in which this book
comes together without Bailey's dedication and effort.

KALI WHITE VANBAALE IS ONE OF my best friends and one of
the earliest contributors to *Past Ten*. We met back in 2012,
climbing into an airport shuttle, clouds of condensation rising
from our breaths as we introduced ourselves on a cold winter
evening in Vermont. We were on our way to start our first year
of graduate school in Montpelier. Later, arriving at our residence
hall, I helped carry her luggage up three flights of stairs. Kali
quickly became a kind of sister in writing. Often, when I have
felt adrift, Kali has been a guiding light. Again and again, she
has helped me carry and sort through my own baggage.

Kali was my first choice when I needed help with the expan-
sion of *Past Ten*. I'm thankful she said yes and stepped in to help
curate this series. Kali's work has helped steer *Past Ten* in new
directions. Once she was onboard, I shared with her my goal
of pulling together a *Past Ten* collection in print. She believed
in the value of the project moving beyond the internet, and
together we began charting a new course for these narratives.

NOT LONG AFTER STARTING past-ten.com, I saw its potential as a book. I liked the idea of *Past Ten* becoming something physical, something people could hold, carry. Kali shared my belief that a print *Past Ten* collection could reach more people. Together with Bailey, we read through every piece published trying to identify themes. We also sought out new writing exclusive to the book. Our hope is that *The Past Ten* might be a map for others to follow to a deeper understanding of themselves. For every contributor to this book and those readers who pick up this work, I wish for them to find a sense of meaning in their journey. I wish for them to find comfort in these pages, like a following wind caught in a sail pushing against the tide of time. This project has taught me how to carry on and make stronger strokes forward. In response to the question of "Where were you on this day ten years ago?" I and others continue to find reasons to keep living.

—Dr. Donald E. Quist
Creator of *Past Ten*

INTRODUCTION

THE MAGIC OF *PAST TEN*

Several years ago, my dear friend and fellow writer Donald Quist asked me to write a micro essay—one thousand words or less—for this unique web journal he was launching called *Past Ten*. He sent a brief explanation of what the journal was about, and how each essay was designed to answer one simple question: "Where were you on this date ten years ago?" Then, he gave me a date to write about: January 11, 2007.

It was just a random date he chose to launch the journal in January of that year, and he had no way of knowing where that date fell in the chronology of my life, or what I might write about. When I did the math and went back in time ten years, I was surprised to find that January 11th was just a few months before I was set to travel to India to complete the adoption of my daughter, a two-year-old toddler whom I had not yet met. Writing about this date, the experience of meeting her for the first time, and the adjustment to life with this new family addition brought up memories and emotions I hadn't thought about in a long time. What started out as writing a little essay as a favor to a friend turned into a profoundly eye-opening, almost magical experience. Seeing the ten-year journey I'd traveled with my, at that point, twelve-year-old daughter was emotional and cathartic because I was able to reflect upon how different she and I were then compared to how we are now. I saw how much our mother-daughter relationship had grown, deepened, and changed in those ten years from where we'd started as strangers brimming with fear and anxiety.

Having had such a moving experience in writing a *Past Ten* essay myself, I eventually joined Donald as a *Past Ten* co-editor, and later with his life partner, Bailey Gaylin Moore, our small team went to work curating new essays for upcoming issues, and developing a book idea. Just as Donald had done, we reached out to friends and acquaintances who we thought might be interested and gave them a random date we were looking to fill in the next edition. And just like what happened with me, time and again, contributors responded that the date we gave them just so happened to be during something profound they were going through in their life at that time. And they, too, found the experience of writing their essay to be profoundly eye-opening and cathartic.

Sometimes we give a date to someone who we know has a great story to tell from that time in their life, but more often than not, it's just a date we randomly choose. The results, though, are still the same; something magical happens, and people open up in ways that keep surprising us. They'll tell us deeply moving, honest, and raw stories about whatever it was they were working through in their life, and, to their surprise and even pride, how different they are ten years later. One way or another, they got through it, time went on, and so did life.

And that's the magic of Donald's *Past Ten*. We are all working through something in our lives, at any stage, at any time. And we get through it, one way or another, to see what surprises another ten years may bring.

—Kali White VanBaale
Managing Editor-at-Large of *Past Ten*

CONTENTS

JANUARY

"LOOKS BROKEN"

Amanda Hadlock

On January 1st, I wake up with two black eyes. I am thirteen years old, and three nights a week I walk to the Assemblies of God church. It's a few blocks away from the duplex where I live with my mother and brother in a suburb of Kansas City, Missouri. I am not religious, really, especially in the speaking-in-tongues kind of way, but it's someplace to be besides home.

The previous night, on New Year's Eve, wind scalds my face as I walk to church. I take my shoes off when I get there and leave them along a wall. I am talking to one of the pastors when I hear a friend yell at me, "Hey Amanda, catch!" Just as I turn my head, a shoe hits me square in the face. My nose begins to bleed. My friend rushes over and the pastor runs to get some paper towels.

"Looks broken," says the pastor as I pinch my nostrils. "Can you call your mom to pick you up?"

I tell him my mother and I share a phone, so I'll have to borrow his. He hands it over and I dial my mom a few times to no answer. I have no clue where she is.

This isn't atypical; she has lots of friends she likes to run around with, but I much prefer her being gone all the time to the occasions she invites her friends over. They're all greasy old guys, and they shoot up in the living room while my brother and I play video games upstairs and pretend not to notice. Mom's phone goes to voicemail again, and I hope they're anywhere but back home.

I call my brother next. He says he's out with a friend, but he'll be there soon. I bid the pastor goodbye. He looks at me with a quizzical expression, but I'm out the door before he can ask too much.

My brother shows up with a bag of ice and drives me back to the duplex. Our electricity is shut off again, so I spend the night in the dark holding an ice-filled dishrag to my nose. By the time my mother comes back a few days later, my black eyes have faded. She doesn't notice the new bend to my nose. I'm not sure she ever heard the story. In the next six months, we'll be evicted from that duplex, and my brother and I will move in with friends where we'll stay until we finish high school. I still don't know what my mother was up to all those years.

IT'S DECEMBER, NINE YEARS LATER. My brother and I sit in our living room playing video games. He tells me after a pull from his Coors Banquet that our mom found him at the gas station he manages that morning and said she wants to come over the next day.

I tense up. I haven't seen my mother since our grandfather's funeral three years ago. She disappeared again shortly thereafter, a nice chunk of inheritance money in her pocket. My brother and I had moved away from our hometown to escape the past, but I suppose a person can never fully lose sight of where they come from. A three-hour drive wasn't enough distance to forget our beginnings.

We finally decide it's best if she doesn't come. If we try to keep her a part of the past. It makes us sad—we know she's homeless—but we can only help her as much as she's willing to be helped, which is not at all. We can't put ourselves through that heartbreak again.

That night, sleet taps against my windshield as I drive to an MA cohort member's house. I wonder where my mother is during the drive and hope she's somewhere warm. Later, my friend helps me dye my hair purple. We spend the night filling out MFA applications to programs across the country. *See?* I think to myself. Things have changed, dammit, my purple hair asserts to the world. I'm getting far away and starting over again, no past to hold me back.

I am not the same. And I am not alone.

"PLEASURE ISN'T INFINITE; IT'S BARTERED"

Phong Nguyen

January 4

Ten years ago, I was thirty-five years old, the age of Dante in *The Inferno*, an age which he called "midway through the journey of life." I had just completed the first draft of my first novel, *The Adventures of Joe Harper*, which took its protagonist from *Adventures of Huckleberry Finn* and its structure from *The Inferno* and began with a thirty-five-year-old Joe Harper wandering the Missouri woods at night. The moment when I had completed the draft, I slammed my hand on the table and stood up in the middle of the coffee shop. It felt a bit like swishing a half-court shot on the basketball court when the crowd was all turned the other way.

Marguerite Yourcenar referred to the years between childhood and old age as "a vain commotion, an empty agitation, an unnecessary chaos," and even though I am still within those years now, when I look back at my thirty-five-year-old self I can grasp how small and strange my current strivings will appear from the vantage of history.

January 4

It's a winter Saturday, and I am preparing a talk for the book release of *Pages from the Textbook of Alternate History*, my second story collection, which will be launched at the Kansas City

Public Library on Tuesday the 7th. I send myself an email of the talk, which is full of overwrought explanations about how alternate history stories are, by definition, *not* factual accounts. I worry that some poor soul will be confused at the very idea of counterfactual history, so I anticipate challenges that might arise in the Q&A and create a sort of decision tree for potential responses. I tread lightly when it comes to a story of mine called "Einstein Saves Hiroshima," which is a not-so-thinly veiled call for peace in a nuclear age because I am hyper-aware of living in Truman country, where rationalizations of the use of nuclear weapons on a hundred thousand innocent civilians abound.

I am hunched over the laptop, a familiar posture on weekday mornings when I compose my fiction; but my upper back protests a bit because it expected a break on the weekend. I lift my neck in an attempt at good posture. Thomas Harris said, "Problem-solving is hunting. It is savage pleasure and we are born to it." My crooked back, then, is a casualty of the hunt.

January 4

I'm in the best shape I've ever been in, perhaps the only time in my life that I've been at the recommended weight for my height, 167 pounds and 5'9". I'm still in my mid-thirties, however, and my attempts at hipness are a bit forced: torn jeans, tight black shirt, a beaded choker. I can't help but feel good about the way I look, and that vanity alarms me because I know its underside is self-loathing when the mirror inevitably reflects back something less healthful and youthful and spry.

Marjane Satrapi said "Anything that has a relationship with pleasure, we reject it. Eating, they talk about cholesterol; making love, they talk about AIDS; you talk about smoking, they talk about cancer. It's a very sick society that rejects pleasure." This is what is left unsaid: life consists of trading one pleasure for another. If I take pleasure in a cheesecake, my pleasure in my body might be diminished. Pleasure isn't infinite; it's bartered.

January 4

It is three weeks away from Burns Supper, and I have recently taken on the responsibility of performing the "Tam O'Shanter," a 228-line poem by Robert Burns, for a gathering of new friends in Springfield, Missouri. Every year since then, I've heard this about my recitation: "It gets better every year." Therefore if I play these performances in reverse, it is a deterioration from the snappy delivery with which I will employ the Scots dialect in the year 2024; so that my 2014 performance is likely a muddle of missed lines and awkward pauses, made worse by the liquor sloshing about in my gut, but it feels good because there is nothing else to compare it to.

Strangely, memorizing the "Tam O'Shanter" has become a family activity. My son and my cousin have committed it to memory, and I learned later that my grandfather used to host a Burns Supper at his home in Whitewater, Wisconsin. It is perhaps odd given how ethnically diverse we are that so many in my family have decided to celebrate the Scottish in our heritage in this way.

My brother will visit and join me for the first time at this Burns Supper gathering. In the background of one photo, you can see between us copies of *Pages from the Textbook of Alternate History*, which was just released.

Despite being the most celebrated poet in all of Scotland, Robert Burns lived and died in poverty. Known as the "ploughman poet," he represented the everyman despite his extraordinary genius. According to Mark Twain in *Innocents Abroad*, soon after Robert Burns died, when they laid the foundation of his memorial in Edinburgh, his mother Agnes Broun was said to have visited the site. She looked at the foundation, then looked toward the sky and said, "Ah, Robbie, ye asked them for bread and they hae gi'en ye a stane."

"BIG THINGS, INDEED"

Tyrese L. Coleman

January 11th: I am wearing lingerie when he enters my place. It's late, one, maybe two, in the morning. My booty-call is a co-worker who decided to visit on a whim after several explicit texts. The third guy I'd sleep with at my job, but luckily, the other two have left. We sit on my sofa. Lights low. Television on.

He says, "I've wanted this for a long time."

I act surprised. I lean into him, realizing as we start to kiss, I am already tired.

I'm twenty-six, doing Big Things: $65,000 a year job, benefits, an Acura TSX. I own my own house.

Well, not a house. I have a condo.

Well, not a George-Jefferson-de-luxe-apartment-in-the-sky kind of condo. I own five hundred square feet on the ground floor of an ancient mid-rise. The walls are seafoam green. The bathroom, fish pink. One night, I woke to loud chomping noises and saw a giant rat slim itself flat and slide through an opening beside the heating unit. Around the corner is a Popeyes and a liquor store with a giant statue of a golden bull on top of it, apparently named The Golden Bull. People live in the woods across from my building. A woman was found slain in the graveyard next door, murdered by MS-13 gang members, my neighbors.

Big Things, indeed.

Usually, I'm on Myspace when I'm alone at night. The search queue is my shopping list. Late at night, I am sprawled across my financed couch watching Mary J. Blige sing on VH1-Soul about going down while I finish a bottle of wine, the blue illumination of my laptop screen glowing across my shoulders and face. The screen shows several potential dates, some I will let take me out. And then maybe, if I feel like it, I'll fuck them. Why not? I have my own house.

My dating life is as glamorous as owning this piece of shit condo. I go from one guy to the next, spending most of my nights alone. There's no such thing as the male equivalent of a deluxe apartment in the sky. Just five hundred square feet of ground-level space and dudes who don't call back the next day.

Afterward, my booty-call and I are talking. The sex was bad, but we laugh it off. We have to, we work together.

I rest my head on his shoulder and tell him I'm tired. Tired of big things. He rubs my arm and says he is too. We want a relationship, but not with one another. We agree silently that this is and will always be our only time together, so that ten years later, if or when we see one another again, there will be no awkward silences or weird tension. We are not meant for one another.

When he leaves, I draft my plan for the next twelve months: find God, save money, pay off my undergraduate debt, apply to law school, work on myself. I write in my journal, "None of the goals noted have underlying intentions related to men. No men, Tyrese! This year is all about me! Oh, and work on getting my place together..."

"CONSTRUCTED BY GUILT AND LOVE"

Gwendolyn Paradice

Lately I've been thinking more about what I refer to as the "secret side" of writing: the processes and brainstorming and influences that contribute to our writing but may not be visible to a reader. I've been dwelling on this because of the forthcoming publication of my first short story collection and how, when my editor asked if I wanted an acknowledgments page, I cried for days because of the secret side of the book that I don't talk about. Even though my work is fiction, the book is informed by a woman I'm no longer friends with, and I mourn, with terrible guilt, the loss of our friendship.

After my divorce, I moved to a new city, to a new house, to live with my best friend from childhood, a woman I'd known for almost two decades. The winter Eva moved in, I reveled having her in my house—*our* house—because she was a comfort, a safe space, and a creative individual that inspired me to work. But living together, and entwining our adult lives, also meant revisiting what happened when we were younger: the instances of abuse I witnessed in Eva's life, abuse that sometimes I was also a victim of.

Ten years ago, on January 13th, living with Eva meant I began, again, to share a place and space with her family members that caused trauma. Weekly, we would attend lunch with these family members, and I went because Eva invited me to

8

and because I thought I was some kind of protector or buffer. Slowly, as time passed, I came to understand that the abuse from childhood was still being perpetrated, the mental illness of her mother still putting Eva on edge and affecting how she could move in the world.

I have no training in helping people the way a psychologist or counselor might. I could not, as Eva's emotional state became more erratic, help her. But worse, I thought it was my place to do so. I did not know how to listen without imparting advice. How to live with someone with post-traumatic stress disorder. I did not know how to balance my needs as an individual with her needs as an individual. And so, when she moved out, our friendship started slipping into memory.

In my book that's coming out, almost every young protagonist in those narratives channels either myself or Eva. She stayed with me, even when we were not together, because I could not—and still cannot—comprehend the enormity and ramifications of the extended trauma she endures. She is the secret side of the collection, a book that never would have come into existence if not for her.

In many ways, I feel haunted by the book. Its publication is a co-mingled excitement and dread. A part of me wants to take tremendous pride in this hurdle of publication. Another part of me wants to take the copies I'll receive and leave them in the box they arrive in, stacked in my garage with the Christmas lights I won't put up, the spider-web-coated tools I don't use, and the old box of pictures I no longer look at. But a part of me is also proud because I am still here, and Eva is too, only states away with a life I don't know. As of now, I don't know what to do with the book, constructed by guilt and a love that is still there, only complicated and undercut by the inability to support her *and* me.

Maybe writing my short collection helped me process *something*—I like to think that it did—but the reality is that I don't think this is true. Writing the book was another form of revisiting abuse, was not a form of therapy, and did not act as a way to work through what happened. Everything feels unfinished and unresolved, even as I line edit, collect blurbs, weigh in on cover design, and receive proofs and promotion opportunities. So, what do we do when the writing we produce—nonfiction or fiction—does not settle? Does not become a pathway to understanding? Does not transform us? Does not *help* us? I have no answer here. I can only pose questions that risk non-answers, or many answers, some of which are still too terrible to write.

"I HAD STATUS WITH DELTA"

James Bernard Short

A decade ago on January 18th, I was that Yankee *Bwoy* in Brooklyn, commuting weekly to the Flatbush on Church Avenue, a predominantly West Indian area, eighteen months into realizing the voice-dream-vision that sparked a divergence in my professional goals. I was heavily into the writing thing—doing it poorly, but enthusiastically—and straddling two distinct worlds: Wall Street professional by day; and personal chauffeur to middle school-aged children on the weekends.

I had status with Delta. Terminal 4 at JFK was my second home. On the eve of the great recession, trouble percolated just beneath the surface of an unstable, capital market. Mortgage-backed securities, Lehman and Bear-Stearns would soon become household names. Death had already visited my household, but not with the cutting swath of indiscretion that would so catch me by surprise. My babies were only ten, eight and four. Having children in college was a conceptual paradigm. Swimming lessons, traveling basketball, sleepovers, and birthday parties…that was my reality. My family sheltered under a single roof. I thought I was happily married; had not yet recognized the red alert warning signs, all pointing to the surety of my marital demise.

Ten years on, I am currently not at the place I thought I'd be, for on January 18th, I could not have imagined the upheaval that would come to define my existence. To say my world changed would be putting it lightly; more like somebody blew it up, and

11

I'm still searching for the fragments of my broken pieces. The one bright spot: I'm upright, no longer scrambling on hands and knees. To be fair, it's not as simplistic (or singularly tragic) as it sounds. Passion has overtaken vocation. I'm still writing, and doing a much better job of it. Emerging—more widely submitted than published—but immersed in the literary world in ways I previously didn't have the proper context to fully understand. With the upheaval and uncertainty came awareness and growth. I live alone, and I don't see my children every day. I'm nearing the end of a lengthy process of detachment and disengagement with official status among the ranks of the divorced my next frontier, but the writing continues to be therapeutic. It's allowed me to be more expressive than at any other stage in my life and has spilled off the page to influence personal engagements across the board. Intentional. Vicarious. Eager to speak my truths…or at least, that is the goal towards which I strive; the narrative I'm heavily invested in believing.

In the absence of love, I have loved harder. I own my quixotic tendencies; more appreciative than ever of tender moments and the blessing of being vulnerable with another person. I continue to make it up as I go. My role as a single father of three wasn't one I'd previously considered. But as I reimagine the world and the place I will occupy in it, I'm focused on finding better and more efficient ways to build an oasis inside the chaos.

Back then, I thought I was happy and settled. I've since learned better. I try to apologize when I fuck up. I no longer take things for granted and acknowledge that silence encourages complicity and can be every bit as damaging as overt aggression. Old habits die hard. Bad ones die even harder. Conflict avoidance is the default position, but I've learned that sometimes, real peace is going to cost you something. When the urge to suppress my feelings arises, I know when I'm doing it and am no longer capable of ignoring it. I don't harbor the same fears, but alas, I'm facing new and different ones.

Life's journey is unceasing. My edification continues.

"HAS MY HEART BEEN BEHAVING STRANGELY FOR A WHILE?"

Jacqueline Doyle

I didn't expect to inaugurate the new year with a week in the hospital for my heart. Until that January, my heart was just a literary trope, not a body part in need of repair.

WAS IT ABOUT FIVE YEARS AGO that my husband took me to the Mercy Center in Burlingame, and we had our chakras read? Sort of woo-woo for me, but hey, we live in California. A pleasant woman with short-cropped gray hair raised a crystal on a string over different parts of my body. Swinging the crystal back and forth slowly, she exclaimed with great surprise that she'd never seen a heart chakra that was so open. When I was hospitalized a couple of weeks ago and diagnosed with heart problems, I thought about the chakra reading. Has my heart been behaving strangely for a while? There's probably no connection.

JANUARY. AN ACUPUNCTURIST sent me to the ER. Also slightly woo-woo for me. I'd seen her twice for excruciating back pain and sciatica. An elderly lady with a black wig slightly askew, she spoke so quickly, her English was so limited, and her Chinese accent so heavy that I understood maybe a third of what she was telling me. In our first two meetings, she'd been extremely bossy, lecturing me on bone broth ("beef tenders" is what I heard, and though I kept asking, I had no idea what they were), on dressing warmly (she insisted on two layers of sweatpants), on the limitations of Western medicine, and on the Chinese herbs I should be taking. When she said, before our third meeting, that my pulse was too low to treat me (32 bpm), I didn't understand her at first. We were sitting in her consulting room, surrounded by boxes and suitcases and piles of clothes and at least ten artificial flower arrangements (she had just cleared out the back rooms for painting). "You go to the ER right now," she said, and I wasn't sure how seriously to take her orders. But my husband took me to the ER, and we spent nine hours there before being released with a diagnosis of bradycardia, persistent low heart rate. At the follow-up appointment the next day, my GP did yet another of many EKGs, sent me back to the ER in an ambulance, and checked me into the hospital for a week. Diagnosis: atrial fibrillation and flutter. Greatly increased chances of stroke and heart attack and blood clots. I still haven't accommodated myself to the diagnosis and how I should live now. The first treatment—electric shocks to my heart—didn't work. I'm on a blood thinner. Next up will be an operation where they burn the interior of my heart to create scars. Everything seems like a metaphor for something I can't quite grasp.

BUT TEN YEARS AGO ON January 25th, my heart was fine. I didn't know yet that a medication I'd been taking for years had badly damaged my kidneys. I still had my gallbladder. I didn't feel particularly old, more concerned with my parents' mortality than my own.

A PHOTO FROM December 2013 in the very disorganized file on my computer desktop reminds me that my husband and I were in New York City for Christmas, reveling in the first snow we'd seen in years. I stuck out my tongue to taste the snowflakes. The slippery sidewalks and soft powdery clumps brought back grad school in upstate New York, where we fell in love. The only other photo I find reminds me that I attended my first AWP in February 2014, in Seattle, and that I was in a reading, but I can't remember for what magazine (*Under the Gum Tree* maybe) or what I read. I'd forgotten until now how touched I was to see some of my creative writing students in the audience. I search my university files for winter 2014 and discover that I was teaching three classes; a creative nonfiction workshop, a literary survey on American women's literature, and a seminar on twentieth-century American drama.

I WAS WRITING, PRODUCING CREATIVE nonfiction and flash fiction after years of doing literary scholarship, and I'm amazed at how prolific I was. It felt like a gift, how the inspiration flowed. The writing group I'd joined in San Francisco took me out of academia into a brand-new place—freer, more fun. That year I published essays on the caregiver who swindled my mother, my mother's dementia, her death, my parents' marriage, my aunt's life and suicide, among others. I'd started publishing the flash that would become my chapbook *The Missing Girl*. I was also planting the seeds for my current work-in-progress, *The Lunatics' Ball*.

JANUARY 25, 2014 IS A SATURDAY, so I am probably working on a flash or an essay. Probably also reading for my classes, jotting notes in the margins of *Death of a Salesman* or *Sula*, though I've taught both of them many times. Perhaps I'm looking over the reading journals from my creative nonfiction students, maybe their first exercise—on "perhapsing" the details they can't fully remember. They find the concept of "perhapsing" and speculation easier to wrap their heads around after we talk about the examples from Maxine Hong Kingston in Lisa Knopp's craft essay in *Brevity*, and essays like Kelly Carlisle's "Physical Evidence" in the *Touchstone Anthology*. During class this week they worked in groups on "perhapsing" with family photographs, getting to know each other, getting to know the possibilities of the genre. The resulting exercises are some of my favorites of the semester.

IT'S A SATURDAY, so our son probably took the BART home from San Francisco with a bag of laundry he's now washing and drying. The Maytag is churning and clanking, the dryer is tumbling, the dishwasher is humming. He's probably out in his room behind the detached garage on his laptop, my husband is working in his study, I might be working in mine, overcrowded with books and folders and papers, but probably I'm on the couch in what we call our sitting room—a converted porch at the front of our small house surrounded on three sides by large windows. Let me guess that it's raining today, silvering the branches of the two enormous fir trees in the front yard. Mist obscures the foothills in the distance. The house feels particularly snug and cozy. My heart swells. I'm enjoying my work and being surrounded by family.

IT'S RAINING NOW, January 2024. I'm still surrounded by family but I'm no longer teaching. Instead, I work part-time as the creative nonfiction editor at an online literary magazine, fulfilling work that I never anticipated. I'm still in the same bimonthly writing group in San Francisco (who imagined we'd be going strong for over ten years!), but we switched to Zoom during the pandemic. Our members have scattered. We'll remain online.

OUR SON WORKED IN San Francisco for seven years before going to Scotland for a graduate degree in environmental science last year. He's leaving tomorrow for Borneo, where he's landed a good job. He plans to stay there indefinitely. We'll Skype often, of course, but it's so far away to visit. Is my heart misfiring because it's broken? We've been through the empty nest before—a number of times—but this one seems the hardest.

MY HEART FLUTTERS like a trapped bird. I become anxious and nauseous, and it feels like my heart's in my throat. None of the similes are adequate to the muscular organ, bloody and literal, that I've paid so little attention to until now. My heart thumps under my hand on my chest. Fast and then slow, barely detectable, and then fast again, throbbing. I check my pulse reading on the Fitbit my son gave me. Check it again a few minutes later and keep checking it because it's alarmingly high. Should I take the med that lowers my heartbeat? Or is it about to plunge on its own? Will I end up in the ER again? It's difficult to swallow. I wonder where I'll be a decade from now. Whether I'll be here at all.

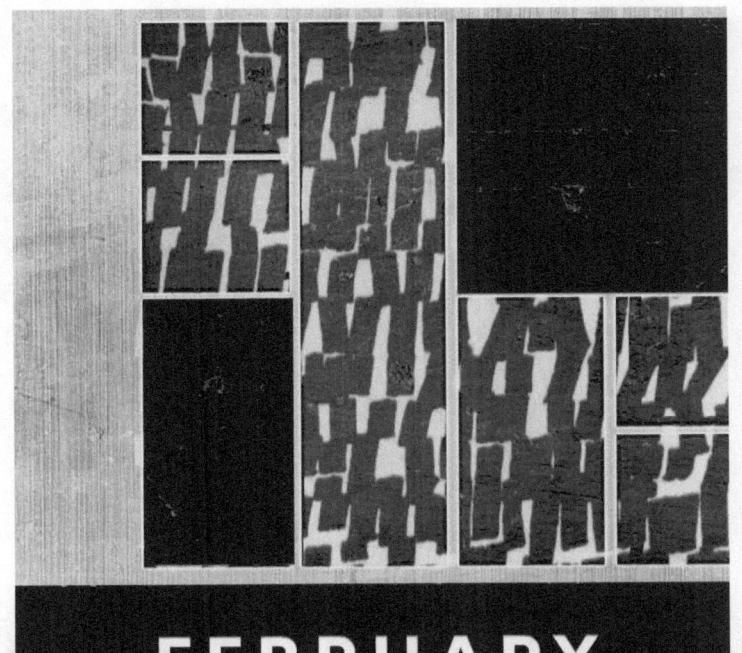

FEBRUARY

"METAMORPHOSIS"

Mathieu Cailler

February 1st; I'm at a friend's house party, bored, not as good with people as I remember being in my early twenties.

Younger me needed the fuel of conversation, but these days I imagine myself as more of a Prius than a gas guzzler, and once I've chatted and laughed and delivered a few stories, I require alone time.

Flanked by a fire pit and a kidney-shaped pool whose water glows a perfect azure, I sip a beer from a local L.A. brewery and pick at the bottle's damp label. These days, I often wonder about my purpose and tell myself there must be more. I'm a writer, but only to myself. Every time I tell people that "I write," and that "I'm working on a story collection titled *Loss Angeles*," they quickly ask if I have ever published something. I list a few obscure journals and some awards, but I can tell they mean *have you ever published a book? Can I go online and get something now?* What mostly happens at these sorts of parties—like half an hour ago actually—is that I share my story, and the person opposite me gets excited, which thrills me, but I soon discover that they only enjoy this conversation because they wish for me to write about *their* life, proceeding to list adventures and mundane anecdotes that have the gravitas and intrigue of a Cheesecake Factory menu.

I sip the last ounce of beer and take a break. I enter my friend's house and descend the stairs toward his bedroom. He's still living at his parents' home, but they are often gone, so he lives something of a *Risky Business* life: always parties, always booze, always noise.

In his room, I plop on the edge of his bed and stare at his bookshelf. There aren't many books, and I recognize all the titles and covers from our high school days together: *A Separate Peace*, *Huckleberry Finn*, *Hamlet*, and *Things Fall Apart*.

On another shelf, though, rests *Metamorphosis*. I have never read this one, and I wonder how it ended up in my friend's room. It looks to be from the local library, and I get up to check the Date Due sticker that is tatted with red, blue, and black stamps. The freshest ink reads "Due Sept 12 1999."

This novel is one of many classics I'm unfamiliar with, and I'm glad to have found it this way—alone, in peace, where I can begin it without hearing *You've never read that!* After the first page, I can tell that I'm going to read this book differently than most people, far removed from the way Kafka intended. I see the words and work as possibility—something can change and change abruptly. One night, a person can go to bed a certain way, and in the morning, awaken a different creature entirely. It's okay that parties like this one, ones I used to crave, no longer fill me with joy. It's okay to pine for my work to be read and enjoyed. It's okay to think that maybe I no longer want to be single, that after years of pushing toward writing, I can be human, soak in sun, yearn for skin and lips, and find someone with whom to share this life.

We evolve, we move, we turn into beetles sometimes.

IT'S BEEN TEN YEARS, and I have changed many times since then. A consistent and ritualistic molting is now embraced. My book, *Loss Angeles*, was picked up months later and published the following year. Since then, I have been fortunate enough to find homes for six more books: one novel, two children's titles, two volumes of poetry, and another story collection that came out in December of 2023.

Perhaps my greatest writing triumph did not come in the shape of a book, though. On March 8, 2020, I entered a bar in Los Feliz to support a new friend's poetry reading series.

I grabbed a drink, took a seat, and relaxed, happy to see the dozens who had come out on a Sunday for live poetry. A brunette-bobbed woman in high-heeled combat boots—something I had never seen before—took a seat next to me. Since the host of the event struggled to work the microphone and speakers, we had a chance to chat. She told me about her father, her hometown, and karaoke, and I discussed the Lakers big win against the Clippers, writing, and the scary information I had learned about Coronavirus.

Due to dating apps, I hadn't asked a woman for her phone number in years, but I managed, and checked that ten digits were present multiple times on the way home. After our first real date on March 12th, I drove home in the pouring rain. I spoke with myself, kindly, sincerely: *I think this could really be something.*

And I still think this, even four years later, even though she is now my wife, even though we are about to enjoy a pot of hot coffee together while playing with our cat.

I awaken every day not as an insect but as something else. Something with limbs and hair and warm blood that feels entirely and beautifully human.

"MY LIFE WAS WATCHING AND WAITING"

Renee Brown

Ten years ago, I was much older than I am today. I was twenty-six, the caretaker for my husband who somehow managed to get cancer in his blood.

Ten years ago, I didn't measure time in years. I measured them in days or nursing shifts or fevers. The shorter stays only lasted six or seven days at a time, watching the slow drips of translucent red chemo and then the whiteboard, which proclaimed his white blood cell count plummeting and then slowly rising again. On February 5th, we were at the hospital finishing up Nathan's last round of consolidation before his bone marrow transplant in March.

Chemo is a poison. It's necessary; they have to use it to kill the cancer cells. But chemo kills cancer because it's killing the person, too. Nathan went to sleep at three p.m. on Tuesday and slept until two a.m. Thursday morning. Twice, he woke up just enough to barely eat something. Both times he threw it back up moments later. He had a headache, muscle stiffness, and then on Wednesday, a fever as well.

After thirty-six hours of watching him sleep and holding my breath whenever it seemed to take too long for him to breathe in again, he felt much better, and so did I. His symptoms were gone, his body temp back down to 98.4. But the doctor on call—not our doctor, but a different oncologist—wanted to run a test just to be sure. She called it a "lumbar puncture test." Everyone else called it a spinal tap.

His spinal tap came back completely clear, but he wasn't able to eat beforehand, so by Friday afternoon, he'd had one small meal in four days. I went and got celebratory chicken nuggets. We watched whatever we could find on the tiny hospital TV that hung from the ceiling—a million miles away from the bed he barely left and my plastic couch in a dull teal shade.

There is a lot I can remember in sharp detail, and a lot that blurs together from the hospital stays. Hospitals always smell the same—rubbing alcohol and cheap antibacterial soap. Unless you are in the children's areas, every hue has been turned down, so as to not be disrespectful. The walls, the floor, the ceiling, the doors, are all eternally beige and white. The only bright colors come from your home: the red and white heart pattern of a blanket my grandmother crocheted for my high school graduation, the blue of a pillowcase so they would know not to take it when changing linens.

I know someone commented on his amazing attitude, though I can't tell you the exact words. I know the times he woke up during his long sleep I had to cajole him to eat, but I can't tell you what it was he tried to eat to make me feel better. Half a bowl of Cheerios? Carnation Instant Breakfast? I know he smiled that stunner, which charmed me from the very first, though I can't remember what he joked about. I know that I loved him with the fierceness of first love, first forever. Ten years ago, my life was only watching and waiting. I thought I was waiting for our life to restart after this detour. Death was not a possibility.

I was wrong. We didn't have another whole year. Nathan had just celebrated his last birthday—twenty-five. One year in the future, on February 4th, we buried the most beautiful, passionate, kindest man I'd ever had the privilege to love, and on this day I returned to an echoing apartment and a grief so overwhelming I had to physically hold myself together when I cried.

Anyone who tells you that grief is just a mental process hasn't grieved, not yet. Grief is a hole somewhere between your heart and your stomach. It goes straight through your core, and it hurts. It hurts worse than corneal erosions, a migraine, or waking up from emergency gallbladder surgery with not enough morphine.

But grief isn't an ending for the living. It goes along with you as you continue. I love Nathan, then and now. In the ten years, I've added Jason to my love. A second forever that's lasted longer than my first.

Cancer can make you ashamed to be enthusiastic about silly things, things that aren't life and death and white blood cell counts. Ten years ago, cancer forced me to be an Adult with a capital A. Now my age is larger, but I'm not nearly so old. Now I am unabashed for the things I had no time to love while I was watching and waiting. Glitter. Rainbows. Unicorns. I've seen enough beige for two people's lifetimes.

"FAILURE FELT LIKE A NEW WAY OF BEING"

Amy Lee Lillard

Here's the thing about failure; the stories we tell portray failing as a necessary step in an upward trajectory towards success, even stardom: the many soul-crushing auditions before an actress wins her Oscar; the disastrous gigs to empty rooms before a band makes platinum; the hundreds of rejections a writer gets before earning that Booker. But failure in the moment rarely feels like progress.

Ten years ago on February 13th, or very close to it, I declared myself a failure at the ripe age of thirty-one. And that declaration felt final. It felt like forever. I was a failure, and that would be my noun and adjective and verb for my future.

I probably woke up cold and stiff on that day, sleeping next to our Chicago condo's poorly packed brick walls.

I probably brushed past my partner of eight years while wolfing down cereal. We didn't talk as easily as we used to, and we argued with a frequency that was, at the time, record-setting.

I probably wore sweats and got a bit sweaty while checking my inbox. I worked as a full-time freelance copywriter for magazines and marketing firms. My clients were dying, one by one, killed off by the one-two punch of the market collapse in 2008 and publishing's slow decline.

I probably put in a couple of hours on existing paid projects, but not enough to cover the month's bills. So, I probably spent some time staring out the window, paralyzed.

I probably reread the latest pages I'd written in my novel. This was the fourth or fifth iteration of this novel, in as many years. I probably felt that sense again, that growing knowledge that this iteration, like those before it, was shit. And since I couldn't figure out how to make it not-shit, I wasn't cut out for this thing I'd wanted to do since childhood.

I probably cried, or tried to. For years I'd convinced myself that the numbness of overmedication was better than the depths of depression.

That night I probably ate, and watched a show on TiVo, and played with our cat, and did all the weekday routines you create as an adult. And during that time, I probably thought about failure. In the moment, failure felt like a new way of being, a sentence for life.

And probably, knowing the future wouldn't have helped because there would be more failure in the next handful of years, as I'd leave my partner, close my business, drink to problematic levels. I'd blow my life up, moving cities and jettisoning the past.

In the moment of real failure, nothing else can be seen. Even if I'd known that by forty-one I'd be surrounded by amazing friends and family, own a house, have a creative writing degree and some publications and an agent, feel content and satisfied in a way I never have before, failure was all I could see.

That's the thing about failure. Although it's a finite step in the process of living, it feels like forever.

"A TIME OF *NOT YETS*"

Caitlin Kunkel

For me, February 18th is a time of *not yets*. In five months I'll be engaged, and in fourteen I'll be married. But not yet.

I'm in Chicago. In fifteen months, I'll be gone, headed to the Pacific Northwest with that new husband to begin the freelance stage of my career. But not yet.

I'll join Twitter in June, where I'll be able to talk to writers and people from all over the world (and waste lots of time along the way). But not yet—now, my life is mostly local and in-person.

Now, ten years later, I live in a studio apartment where I can walk to the lake. I'm so close to the train that I hear the station announcements in my bed, the exact same recorded intonation every ten minutes. I set my alarm for 5:15 a.m. on weekdays so I can watch my Netflix DVDs and mail them back on the way to work. Very soon, that sentence will sound unbearably dated. But not yet.

I work in fundraising, the only job I could find after the financial crash. The work is easy, and very quickly I get to experience that strange sensation of being good in a field you don't want to advance in. I learn how to produce events, keep meticulous records, speak easily and jovially to people who I don't know or care about. I talk on the phone, send emails, write in a voice not my own, ask for money, make small talk, and get incredibly bored. Eventually, I'll need all these skills for another job, one that I do care about. But not yet.

I've recently emerged from five years of insomnia, and a problem with sleeping pills. The insomnia will return, but blessedly, not yet. Now, I wake up after an entire night's sleep and feel euphoric, strong, superhuman.

Every day during lunch I take my tiny computer and go to the mezzanine of the ravenous theater I raise money for, and I write. A novel? Not yet. Satire? Not yet. I write short character monologues, trying to understand how to be funny on the page. I keep a very literal blog called "Caitlin's Characters" and I write one per day. Ten years ago, I could have been writing from the perspective of a sister who's suffered an absurd loss, or a choirboy terrified that his voice is changing, or even a lamp who hates being turned on. They aren't connected, and they serve no larger purpose other than teaching me how to trust that there will always be more ideas in my head. Because I'm not over that fear, yet.

I take comedy classes at night and make an entirely new set of friends. We produce our own shows, very seriously slotting ourselves into the roles of producers, directors, marketers. In seven months, I'll be a comedy writing teacher myself, a profound step in shaping the arc of my career, but for now, I'm a beginner, a novice, a student.

I don't have a Google calendar (yet), and my paper planner contains my life. I carry bags and bags around the city with me; stuffed with days of gym clothes, work clothes, "fancy" clothes for work events, books, pajamas, makeup, swimsuit, goggles, bike shorts, my computer, and sheaths of printed out sketches. It's not unusual for me to carry four bags all day on public transit to five or six different locations between 6:30 a.m. and 10:30 p.m. Eventually, I'll get tired of this, of being so transient. But not yet.

Now, I love walking into the big, institutional theater where I work. I love walking into the tiny, filthy comedy theaters where I produce shows. I love showing up at the Chicago storefront theaters after work and seeing plays that make me want to go right back to my little computer and work on my characters, the very first building block of writing longer things myself. It takes years to eventually realize that I'll never see as much theater as I did during that time. But I don't know that, yet.

There are things coming soon that I'm building the foundation for on February 18th. I don't know what they are, because on that day, I have no idea what shape I want my life and career to take. But wonderfully, I don't have to know, yet.

"IT HURTS TO PUT MY SHOES ON"

Kathy Fish

It's a bright, Colorado winter's day on February 25th. The Ponderosa pine trees that line my back fence are half the size they are now, their branches mittened with snow. I am at my desk, a blanket over my lap, going over edits on my second book, a collection of stories I no longer feel connected to. It's as if they were written by someone else and in a sense, they were. The chronic, debilitating pain I'm experiencing will last nearly two years, and no one outside my doctor and my immediate family will know about it. I am certain this will be the last book I publish.

MY TEENAGE DAUGHTER asks if I feel well enough to take her shopping. I'm shocked by the question. Is this how she sees me? A mother too fragile to take her to the mall? *Of course,* I tell her, determined not to let her down. It hurts to put my shoes on. In every store, I claim the chair outside the dressing room like an old person or a husband.

THE PAIN IS CONSTANT yet flickering. It travels through my body the way Christmas tree lights twinkle on and off. First my hands, then my elbows, a knee. Pain stabs my left temple, then it's my shoulder, my toes. My doctor is nodding, writing HYPOCHONDRIAC in my chart. *What a terrible description,*

I tell her. *Haha! Some writer,* I say, trying to appear sprightly and self-deprecating and not crazy.

I DREAM WE'VE MOVED into a filthy, dilapidated house. The rooms are tiny and filled with old clothes. The floors slope. A lightning-shaped crack zig zags across the ceiling. Outsized rodents roam the halls. There's no going back. This is a done deal. I'm already resigned to living here for the rest of my days.

I CAN FAKE IT WHEN I NEED TO, and I need to a lot. Fun things, events, outings are a distraction I can temporarily enjoy. We take a family trip to Spain, but I grow more exhausted each day. I'm wearing the same long sweater in every photo, the sleeves pulled down over my hands. I fall behind as we climb a cobblestone hill and my son runs back and takes my arm. I am a hundred years old. One night we go to a flamenco show in a cave bar in Granada. The singer's voice wails, keens, like nothing I'd heard before. There I am in the front row, sobbing, as some grief I don't understand and cannot name erupts inside me. It embarrasses the hell out of my kids.

I CRY OFTEN and without warning. My doctor orders a nerve conduction study. I'm told the electricity delivered through the electrodes to my nerves will only cause mild tingling, but for me, it's excruciatingly painful. The neurologist says he's never made anyone cry before and I apologize. All my life I've tried to be a good patient and good patients don't complain, and they don't cry. The test comes back normal, like all the other ones. I feel embarrassed, guilty. There are people who are truly sick in the world. I'm wasting everyone's time.

JUNG BELIEVED THAT IN DREAMS a house symbolizes the self and that the unconscious is always seeking outward manifestation. A broken-down house is a sign of something broken within. My dream was a warning.

FINALLY, I TAKE MATTERS into my own hands. I begin meditating, become scrupulous about my diet, unfurl my dusty yoga mat. Gradually, I start to feel better. I no longer wake up stiff and sore. Gradually, I start to write again. I go for longer and longer stretches of clear headedness. Actual ideas form in my brain. The creative impulse returns. I come back to myself.

I WISH I'D HAD A CRYSTAL BALL then and could see my life as it would be ten years later. I didn't know, didn't dare allow myself to believe, that I would go on to write more stories and publish more books. Or that I would discover a passion for teaching, and it would bring me so much joy. Whatever "it" was, I came out of it. I know not everyone does. If I gained anything from my two years of struggling with an invisible enemy, it's empathy for those who live with chronic illness. If that's you, you have my heart and my compassion. I hope you get answers and relief and brighter days ahead.

"HOW TO REMEMBER A DAY THAT DIDN'T EXIST"

Ryan Collins

My Uncle David, who was a children's author, was born on a leap year: February 29, 1940. I grew up hearing my father complain about how, three out of every four years, my uncle would bellyache about "not having a birthday" that year, guilting their family and friends into a week of birthday happenings and extra gifts. And then, on that fourth year, he'd milk the occasion as his only chance to *really* celebrate for another four years. My uncle died unexpectedly when he was sixty-one (or fifteen-and-a-quarter, if you count his "actual" birthdays).

Ten years ago was not a leap year, and so there was no February 29, 2014. So, how to remember a day that didn't exist? What was I doing at that time, when it would have been February 29, 2014? Would the closest day be February 28? March 1? Neither date seems correct or feels right. How does one account for such a liminal space in the calendar—the line between 2/28 and 3/1 becomes more a crevasse into which possible days might fall. Who would notice they're missing if no one is looking for them?

Around February 29, 2014, I was in Seattle for the Association of Writers & Writing Programs Conference (AWP). I had received a small grant to help offset travel expenses and attended some panels relevant to my work as the Executive

Director of the Midwest Writing Center (MWC), a small literary arts nonprofit that my Uncle David helped found in 1980.

Prior to attending, I was invited to participate in the seventh installment of the Dusie Kollektiv, a series of self-produced chapbooks collected and hosted by the journal/press Dusie. All the participating authors got together for a reading during the conference, and it felt great to be around so many other poets. I attended a strange brunch reading with some of my favorite writers, as well as several other readings and events with friends and writers I admired. I was also invited to read at another off-site reading, one with a lineup so packed with notable and award-winning names on the bill, my being included seemed like a lucky mistake. This proved to be a highlight of the trip and of my writing life to date.

When I arrived at the venue (a large bar/restaurant in Pike's Place Market, packed Friday night patrons and poets lining the aisles, creating havoc for the front-of-house staff), I noticed two things: 1. most if not all of the patrons appeared to have no idea there was going to be poetry reading during their dinner, and 2. I couldn't really hear the readers over the din of conversation and noise of a full Friday night dining room.

I was also told by one of the hosts that I was "on stage" in two minutes. I had just enough time to get a couple of poems ready while the host read my bio. I stood up next to a table of six people, perplexed and trying to enjoy their meals, when the organizer gave me the mic and a single instruction: "Be fucking loud." I took this to heart.

I could tell I was loud enough when nearly every head I could see in the room turned as soon as I belted out the title of my first poem, "What You Need." My near shouting felt like it focused the attention, and it seemed like the patrons turned down a bit when I turned up, so to speak. It stayed that way for my three poems, and for the rest of the reading.

Afterward, I was sitting at the bar with a friend when a well-known poet approached me, said he really dug my poems, especially the first one, and asked if I would send it to him for the magazine he was editing. I expressed my gratitude, being a tremendous fan of his, and not being accustomed to such acknowledgements or invitations. When I returned home, I sent the poem to him, as requested, and he published it—the poem became the opening poem in my first book, which was picked up for publication later in the summer of 2014.

NOW, TEN YEARS LATER, I'm finishing writing this, having just returned home from AWP in Kansas City. While this year was an entirely different experience (I worked a table at the book fair for work—no readings, no chance encounters pointing toward publication), I was still fortunate to learn and be inspired by a wealth of terrific writers. I was able to see many friends I'd not seen since before the start of the pandemic.

I admit to feeling worried about attending this year before I went, reflecting on ten years ago and feeling like my writing has slipped down a crevasse, through a slot in time. Shouldn't I have more happening around my work? It feels like ten years ago was a bracketed space, a leap into a time that existed outside of the calendar. Though unlike birthdays (for most of us, at least), not every year is ours to celebrate, and bellyaching doesn't manifest any joy or occasion—it pushes them away.

Time is a puzzle box we've trapped ourselves in, and ten years removed from my magical days in the Emerald City, I'm struggling to find certainty or instruction about what happened then, and how it matters, or doesn't, to me now. But it's okay. I am grateful to be here writing, thinking about this in-between day, and my Uncle David, the liminal spaces where he might be, where we find ourselves in time. These spaces are where poems are born.

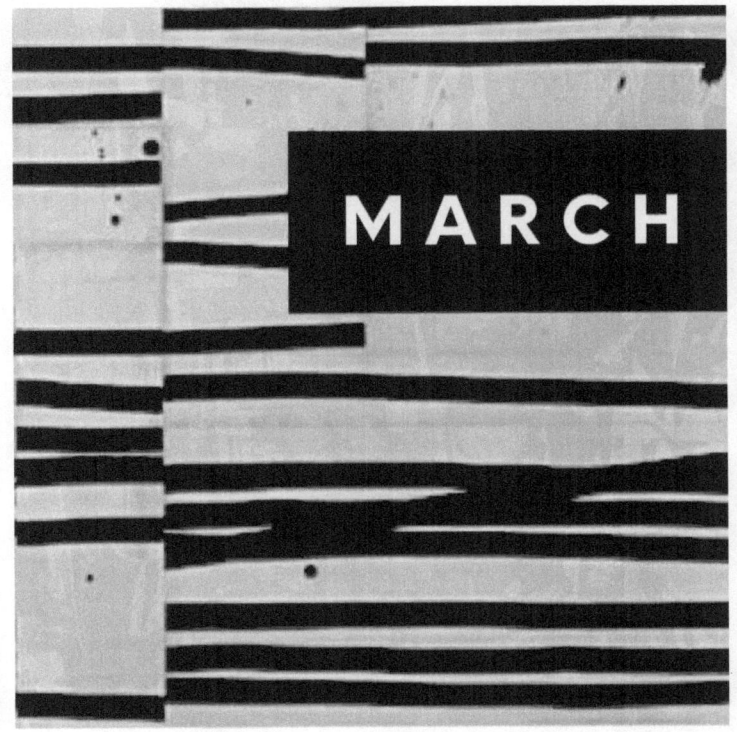

MARCH

"BEING DEAD WAS EASY, BEING LEFT BEHIND WAS HARD"

Ann Dávila Cardinal

We had just returned from celebrating my fiftieth birthday in Puerto Rico. Ten days filled with laughter, conversations, and dancing with family and friends, lost in the nurturing, starchy embrace of fried plantain, the minty-lime taste of mojitos still on our tongues. On March 2nd, as we settled back into our routines in Vermont, I saw the monumental birthday as a push to help me jump into the next decade with both feet and a renewed focus on building a writing career. Our son Carlos was sixteen, busy with sports, school, and friends, and it was time for me to really dig into my craft.

My husband's colonoscopy the next day was nothing more than an item on our post- vacation to-do list. A few months earlier I had found a coffee-stained letter on the kitchen counter telling Doug it was time to get a colonoscopy. When I asked him about it, he waved it off. "I'm too busy right now." To which I responded, "Oh *hell* no," and made an appointment for when we got back. But there we were, trying to catch up after vacation, and both of us lamented the interruption to our lives. On the way to the hospital, Doug groused, "This growing old thing is a pain in the ass."

That afternoon I left work early to pick him up at the hospital. I was going to bring him home and then have drinks with a friend while he slept off the anesthesia. But when I checked in at radiology, I was told the doctor wanted to talk to me. Confused, I followed the nurse to recovery where the doctor was talking to a still groggy Doug. I wasn't worried yet, but it felt weird, like it was happening to someone else. "Mrs. Cardinal, as I was just telling your husband, I'm afraid it's cancer. We'll be making you an appointment with an oncologist."

No, wait.

I had obviously stepped into some film plot, something probably starring Julia Roberts and filled with overwrought and emotionally manipulative tropes. I stared at the doctor, weirdly focused on how the hairs of his white eyebrows hung over his eyes like awnings. "No. Not possible. How can you know that? Don't you have to do a biopsy?" Clearly, the man was an idiot.

"I've been doing this long enough that I can assure you it is. We won't know if its spread to his lymph nodes until we do the surgery—"

"Surgery?" My mind skittered to catch up, running on the ice of his words, unable to find purchase. I looked down at Doug all tucked in under his warmed hospital blanket, smiling, forearms crossing each other as if he were rehearsing for the coffin. I wanted to pull his hands apart and shake him. What are you smiling about?

The doctor saw me looking at him. "He still has anesthesia in his system. He probably doesn't really understand yet."

"Oh, he understands." I knew that for Doug, this wasn't a crisis. If our roles were reversed? He'd be a mess, but I'd learned long ago my husband didn't fear his own death much, perhaps from his abusive childhood, perhaps from flirting with it so many times in his rough and tumble rural Vermont childhood. But my death? Our son's? Those terrified him. Being dead was easy, being left behind was hard.

We gathered his things, took our paper of instructions and upcoming appointments, and drove home in a daze. Later that afternoon, when our Carlos came home from basketball practice, we sat him down and told him what we knew. When you are a family of three, there are few secrets. With a lean familial unit, each member feels the emotional eddies of the other two, getting pulled into the wake of triumphs and crises alike, whether you want to or not. We faced this together with tears, laughter, misplaced anger, and a fuckload of love.

WE CALLED IT THE YEAR that cancer took, but even though it had spread to his lymph nodes (stage three colon cancer), damned if it was going to find Doug's cranky-ass body hospitable. Despite smoking a pack of unfiltered cigarettes a day, he was fit and wasted zero time feeling sorry for himself. He was pissed when on chemo days when they told him he couldn't go to work. He shoveled the snow for the disabled neighbors with an infusion pack strapped to his chest, poison being continuously fed into the port they'd installed under his skin. Me? I spent every lunchtime writing in the college library, banging away at a horror novel, feeling like that hour was sacred, it was mine and mine alone. Well, as it turns out, the cancer didn't have a chance in my "hey-you-kids-get-off-my-lawn" husband, and a year later he was declared cancer-free.

IN THE TEN YEARS SINCE, both my son and I faced our own battles with near-death illnesses, but both of us survived, making the three of us even more resilient, stronger as a family and as individuals. Today, having just celebrated my sixtieth birthday with friends and family, I am writing this from the balcony of my uncle's condo in Luquillo, Puerto Rico, the sound of the waves a constant accompaniment to the words on the page. The funny thing is, with all we went through, my writing flourished. In the last ten years, I've written seven novels, four short stories, and three scripts, and Carlos and I are now writing scripts together. I have learned more about the craft and the business of writing than I ever imagined possible and feel buoyed by an outstanding community of writers who love and support each other. Last month I left my job of twenty-four years to give a go at writing full time.

HOW IS DOUG THESE DAYS? No recurrence of cancer (knocking wood as I type). Of all the things I've learned in the last ten years about the craft of writing, about family, our bodies and health, about life, it's this:

Growing old might be a pain in the ass, but it is so much better than the alternative.

I LOOK FORWARD to seeing where I am in March of 2033. See you then?

"ONE DAY SHE DIDN'T TURN UP"

Anu Kumar

Ten years ago, on March 8th, a day when the world's women celebrate themselves, Morgina did not turn up to work. Not at her usual time, not even an hour later.

Earlier that year, we had moved from crowded, cosmopolitan Mumbai (always Bombay to me, and not merely for the name's nostalgic value) to Gurgaon, near Delhi. Bombay was where I worked for a liberal magazine, a place I loved. However, I still had an open mind about Gurgaon, a town that had leapfrogged to medieval modernity. It had all the world's IT companies, glitzy malls, and high-rise buildings with state-of-the-art security systems.

Every so often, especially on slow-moving summer afternoons, vile dust danced up from hills in the west and weaved through Gurgaon's streets. The dust seeped through windows, snaked past every available gap; it arranged itself in fine grainy layers on furniture, especially bookshelves, and left a brown layer on everything exposed. One needed a domestic helper to tame the dust, and Morgina had already worked for us for two months before the day she vanished.

Morgina was "sent" to me by a neighbor.

"She works for me in the mornings, but she can come over to yours for an hour. You don't have much to clean, since it's just you and your husband, but make sure you give Morgina enough work to fill that hour." My friend added that I must never allow the *maids* to feel too important. Calling them *domestic helpers* was quite unwise. "Monitor her. If you are casual, these people will see through you and adjust accordingly. They are flexible that way."

My friend instructed me to negotiate the salary. "If Morgina's going to come to work for you on the tenth or any date, pay her on a pro-rata basis, and only pay her on that date."

Besides these rules, there was advice: do not completely believe their stories. Their excuses could be fiction. And one must never get too friendly with them. It's all about getting them to do the work.

I forgot these warnings when Morgina didn't arrive for work the first time. When Morgina did appear, two days later, calm and nonchalant in the manner I had come to associate with her, she told me her husband had been picked up by the police. Morgina's husband was a rickshaw puller and he ventured out only in the afternoons after Morgina had returned from working in other people's apartments. Morgina's husband had no money to give the police for their weekly bribe. The police were insistent, she said. If he didn't pay them the "hafta," they threatened to arrest him as an illegal immigrant from Bangladesh.

"When the police do that, we are helpless," Morgina said. "We don't have papers or ration card. We never had money to stand in line. And the man who can stand in line for rations demands money. Someone ran away with our money."

I felt guilty for not paying Morgina her salary earlier. It could have saved her husband from police harassment. I gave Morgina the money so she could get someone to stand in line for her ration card. After that, Morgina never seemed to run out of stories. She began to linger after work every day. She gossiped, telling me about how a little girl in another flat followed the servants around in every room, monitoring them; how a husband and wife quarreled in another house, and the way a mother-in-law nagged her son's wife constantly in another home. I reciprocated by telling Morgina about her namesake, the clever helper from the Arabian Nights' story of *Ali Baba*.

Perhaps working for a left-leaning magazine taught me to appreciate the unexpected stories that come my way from such chance encounters. Maybe that is why I broke every rule and ignored all advice when it came to domestic helpers. My apartment was unquestionably the dustiest, something in-laws frowned over and found fault with.

Morgina left suddenly. One day she didn't turn up. After a while, when she still hadn't returned, I knew she never would.

"The police told Morgina and her husband to go," I heard a friend say.

"Some maids went to the other new high-rise which offers better pay," said another.

All stories about Morgina were somehow incomplete. But I feel sure Morgina's story was, and is, happy. Since then, I've learned to accept—and to love—incomplete stories and all the possibilities they contain.

"MARCH 11TH, OR, I SAID GOODBYE TO MY CHILDHOOD DOG OVER ZOOM"

Grae Gardiner

This morning, I don't know
what I'm even mourning.

The withered lab-pit mix
named for the stars and moon

and a children's-book bat
who lost then found family

everywhere. The jagged
ruby-clot of cells I passed

sudden a couple weeks
back to the watershed

or landfill, contingent
to the steps of my local

wastewater treatment plant.
My mood of clouded mirror

its extinguished, endless,
eviscerating lack.

A year or two or ten
of sublimated grief.

A decade ago, I was
seventeen in a schoolroom

vaguebooking pop songs,
sink-or-swimming in all

the wrong christian rules
and academic creeds,

corroding my body's tender
plume of gender for sex,

achingly oblivious
piously repressed

and everyone I've lost
was still alive, somewhere

in the future-past of *not yet*.
Dear teenage-complicity—

Dear un-diary— Dear
one-day-slinks-to-the-next—

I have a headache
the size of a quarter

million obituaries
hurtling exponentially,

a colicky unease
as rampant as the mask-less

as swollen, bitter-rawed
as the gaslit every time
I leave my ramshackle
domestic. I live in

the smallest magnifications
of worry, fury, sadness,

scraping through each day minute-
by-minute. Ultimately, I am scared

I am foolish in my hurt
—harboring. Even to say *why*

or *how* runs on empty.
What can be left

when trauma tangs the air
in persistent erosion. I try,

I am trying to parent
in the radical, unlegal

etymology: to origin
-ate and affect an account

-able stake in this world
I will not shake: to care

for my place. I write out
this unordinary ordinary

because it happened
because it is happening

because no one should be let
to forget or doubt or undo it.

Least of all a future self.
Least of all a current me.

"MY CHILD CAN BE A PENGUIN IF THE OTHER OPTION IS DEATH"

Nikki Boss

March 14th was a Friday. I worked that night, ten years ago. The strip club was my playground. Most of the time, the club was like a big party. We were fake, all of us: nails, hair, noses, boobs. A bunch of messed-up women desperate to be someone else. We'd smoke cigarettes on the porch off the dressing room, bang a few lines, fix our hair, and try not to trip down the stairs back into the club.

I quit dancing near the end of March that year. The transition was hard, the attention and the cash were intoxicating. Also, it was easier to hide behind a stripper identity when I was a single mom with daddy issues.

Church, rehab, and higher education sobered me up. I became fully immersed in Jesus culture. For me, rules + discipline = functional adult. In grad school, I began practicing my own beliefs on myself: love and forgiveness.

During a graduate school residency, I traveled to Slovenia. One night at a bar, nestled in a lounge chair under a covered patio, whiskey glasses and beer bottles littering the table, I entered an intense conversation with a friend and fellow student.

I asked them, and myself, *why am I like this? Why am I so mad?*

They answered simply, something I never could have seen on my own. *Because you've been fighting your whole life,* they said.

Back home I am confused, sad, and desperate. The sermons I hear are becoming opinions borne of fear. I wonder what happened to the book of "Acts" but am too afraid to lose my place, afraid to lose what feels like the only community I have.

My daughter attempts suicide six years later in May. She swallows half a bottle of Valium. She says she is my son now. My child can be a penguin if the other option is death. I call three places where I hold obligations: work, theater, church. The immediate and total support from two of these places is overwhelming but the third, my place of refuge, fails. There is a reaction, not a response. I am told my child is not welcome to interact within the church.

After, a retraction: prayerless, perfunctory, no witnesses despite my asking.

Even the girls at the strip club were better behaved than this. Despite our invented personas, all the manipulation and lies, we at least played by the rules.

I find myself staring at my own Facebook for hours, wondering who I am.

Ten years ago, I forgot who I was. To become what I thought a functional mother and wife should be, I forgot what I stood and knelt for. Ten months ago, the God I love did not align with the God offered to me, and it took me too long to remember that men are not Gods.

I remember when I used to believe I could save the world.

I remember a girl who spoke up when something wasn't right.

Ten years later, I'm discovering her again.

I'm still processing, evolving, and learning. It's hard to know how to love myself. I don't know the answers to too many of my own questions, but I do know that God, the real God, is love. And love will always win.

"I'LL GIVE YOU EDITH WHARTON"

Kevin Prufer

On March 15th, I was going to visit an old friend. He'd grown up in a junkyard out West, and when we first met, he was trying to write poetry and living in a garage in Ohio. He slept on an old door propped up by cinder blocks. He had a twenty-year-old minivan, looked like John Lennon, and had been fired from a lot of jobs. I admired him and I apologized for him, because he spoke his mind and he was a racist. And he mostly didn't like women because, he said, his own mother had twice tried to drown him and once set his car on fire. Sometimes, when we were out drinking, I had to apologize for things he said, but that wasn't hard. No one really wanted a fight. He's drunk, I said, he's just talking. And everyone would calm down and go back to their pool games and drinks.

And he was drunk, a lot. I was, too, when we were together, and I think, most of all, I was amazed by his talent. He wrote like an angel, one of my friends once said of him, and it was true. He was like those people who are born able to draw perfect human bodies, who, from childhood, can sit at a piano and compose sonatas. He understood unerringly how a beautiful sentence might sound and his poems were lush and personal and painful to read.

So, yes, I admired him and when I moved far away, I thought about our evenings in those rural Midwestern bars, the sticky floors and bathrooms with doors that wouldn't quite shut and the smell of beer and the noise of baseball on TV crashing into the noise of an old jukebox, and no one paying attention to either of them.

And my friend drinking bourbon, drunk, composing conspiracy theories about Wordsworth, his voice loud against the noise. Fitzgerald couldn't write for shit. Roth, neither, a pretentious New York Jew. Or: Name one woman novelist who's really important. And by important, I mean *immortal*, he said.

Edith Wharton.

Okay, Edith Wharton. Okay. I'll give you Edith Wharton. But that's it.

Willa Cather.

Okay, sure. That's two. But two's hardly any. Two is almost zero.

Flannery O'Connor.

And then he'd wipe his hair out of his eyes and shake his head and change the subject. He wanted to talk about jazz saxophonists and the industrial revolution and the history of Alaska. He read books, lots of them. He read a book a day, he said.

But on March 15th, I hadn't seen him in a while. I'd moved away five years before. I had a good job at a good university and a nice house in the hip part of Houston, Texas, and my friends were artists and newspaper reporters and college professors and we went to wine bars with clever names and talked about Obama and whatever was showing at the art museum.

Still, I missed the rural Midwest and part of that was my friend who lived in the garage, and on March 15th, I was driving to see him again. He had better digs now, he'd told me, and a job. He'd moved to a city, well, not *city*, exactly, but near a city.

And that's where I found his house, a two-bedroom white ranch with his dirty pickup truck in the driveway. When I pulled my rental car up, he came out into the spring sunlight, the screen door smacking closed behind him. He wore a white undershirt, stained, and he hugged me. He smelled of bourbon and cigarettes and mint and he didn't look like John

Lennon anymore. He looked smaller and unsteady, as if his boots didn't fit.

His house smelled of five years of cigarettes.

You have to move the books away if you want to sit down, he said. And the cat, too. Just move the cat. He won't bite.

You still writing? I asked him.

No, he said. Well, I try. But I've got a lot going on. Lotta assholes at work.

He poured bourbon from an enormous bottle into paper cups. One for him, one for me.

Dust motes swirled and glittered by the windows. One of the cats was batting at an orange peel on the floor.

In the light, his face looked gray, but he smiled broadly. I'm movin' on up, he sang, to the tune of *The Jeffersons*. And he laughed, the liquor bottle in one hand, the paper cup in the other. Like the new digs?

I laughed, too. It was good to see him. Now, he was talking about some great writer I'd never read, and then another I had read, but had mostly forgotten about. It was the same kind of stuff he used to talk about, and he waved his pale arm grandly in the little living room.

Then he was silent for a moment. We both were.

And how're you doing, Mr. Success, he finally asked. Fancy job. Got a good woman at home. Got a fancy book contract. Must be nice, huh?

It's all good, I said.

Art Blakey was playing on the turntable. Thousands of records in wooden crates lined one wall. I could see my rental car through the window behind him, shiny and blue.

My friend considered me.

I'll bet it is, he said.

"I AM CALLING IT AN ASIAN AMERICAN SEX COMEDY"

Pete Hsu

It is March 16th. I am writing a novel. It is the first time I have attempted to write a novel.

My novel is titled *Schlongky Kong*. It is about a woman named Scharlene Kong who is the singer in a rock band called Schlongky Kong. It is set in the 1990's. Scharlene is trying to get famous while also trying to rescue a group of indentured Chinese nationals. I am calling it an Asian American Sex Comedy.

I take a novel writing class titled Novel Writing 3. The school has five levels of novel writing classes. I have not taken levels 1 or 2. I am confident that my work is so good that I do not need to take these earlier levels. But, I am humble enough not to try and take levels 4 or 5. Also, levels 4 and 5 require instructor approval, which I do not have.

I get to work on my novel.

Meanwhile, I visit local seminaries—seminaries are graduate schools for the study of religion. The religion I am interested in studying is Christianity. I grew up in the Christian church. I have mixed experiences with the church—some good, mostly bad. The church's politics have become mostly terrible. A lot of the people in the church have turned out to be fake and also materialistic. But still, Christianity was my first experience of the divine. This is important to me. I get it in my head, if you can't beat them, join them.

I visit an evangelical seminary in Pasadena. It is a somewhat famous seminary. I go on a school tour. There are a lot of people there. They are very friendly people. They are very energetic. They are mostly young and they seem to come from all over the country and also from other countries. The seminary gives me a nice satchel bag for free. They also have a brunch buffet, also free. I confess that I do not think I believe in the literal Christian God anymore, but I still consider myself a Christian person. Nobody likes this. Someone calls me Simon Magus. This is not a compliment. Simon Magus was a sorcerer who wanted to buy the Holy Ghost from the apostles. He is considered a villain.

In my Novel Writing 3 class, I meet the other writers. The teacher has written a novel about a boy leaving his religion. One student is writing a science fiction version of a Faulkner novel. Another is writing a YA version of a Shakespeare play. Another is writing a wildly beautiful coming-of-age novel about a girl in the desert. I like their writing. I also like them as people.

I share my work with the class, my novel's first chapter. This is something I have written and rewritten several times, so it is probably my best work—or, it is at least something I have obviously worked on a lot.

My classmates tell me how much they like it. Also, they tell me that I am good at writing from a woman's point of view. I am flattered but also not surprised because I think I am a really good writer. I do not let it show that I think I am a good writer. I try to act like I do not think I am very good.

My second turn to share my work, it goes differently. My classmates are confused. I have brought in new elements to the story, like track & field and classical quartets. I have not explained these new elements. My classmates do not understand why I have brought in these new elements. Also, I have written a sex scene. My classmates find my sex scene neither sexy nor anatomically possible. I am surprised by their reactions. Also, someone questions whether or not my novel infringes on copyright laws.

Meanwhile, I visit another seminary. It is not an evangelical seminary; it is what they call a mainline seminary. I feel very comfortable there. They seem to be anti-capitalist and believe in LGBTQIA rights, immigration rights and social justice causes. They do not seem bothered that I do not believe in the literal Christian god. They tell me that atheists are welcome to attend their seminary. I like all this. But, there are only about five or six people at the visit, and they are not very energetic. They are also somewhat old. I am somewhat old. I am forty years old, but being forty years old makes me the youngest person there. Also, the buildings are dilapidated.

I decide I do not want to enroll in seminary.

Back in class, I work on my novel some more. I think about what my classmates have told me. I keep writing. My writing seems to get messier but also more entertaining. I like this. It is a strange thing—I feel like my writing is both better and worse than when I started.

As it turns out, my novel *Schlongky Kong* is never completed. I write a draft of it. It is one hundred pages long. It ends with a rescue scene followed by a chase scene followed by a last stand against the evil kidnappers. It seems, by the end, to have nothing to do with the rock band, which is why I wanted to write it in the first place.

But, one chapter from *Schlongky Kong* is good. At least I think it is good. I take it and rewrite it into a short story. I submit it to journals. It is accepted pretty quickly and becomes my first publication.

The rest of *Schlonky Kong* is lost forever when my computer crashes. I did not have the cloud back then. I am not sad about this.

"SO MANY WHO LOOK JUST WANT TO BE SEEN"

Caylin Capra-Thomas

MARCH 20

First day of spring in Missoula, forty-two degrees. I'm twenty-six, and I live alone in the edge-lands between argument and aria: the doomed couple next door's sloshed, cacophonous conflicts and student opera singers downstairs belting scales. But my tiny apartment is quiet today. I'm looking out the window past some new life's astringent greenery towards the still-snowy mountains that hug the town. I'm on the phone. I'm calling a long-term drug and alcohol recovery center in Georgia, where my big brother has been since December. It's his thirty-fourth birthday.

I have always known Curtis was an equinox baby, but I have also always had trouble remembering whether his exact birthdate is the 20th or the 21st. Perhaps this is because the vernal equinox can fall anywhere between March 19th and March 21st, or perhaps it is because I have, as one high school teacher put it, the memory span of a goldfish. Well. Joke's on you, Mr.—. Would a goldfish remember this?

CURTIS ALSO HAD MR.—, who told me he remembered my brother best for having ingeniously taped quiz answers to the front of his own teacher's desk where he couldn't see them.

This was Curtis's reputation—a bright kid who used a lot of his brain power to circumnavigate the rules. I envied him for this. I feared the very whiff of trouble, no matter its object or their guilt. My stomach churned with dread for movie villains getting their comeuppance. At seven, I closely followed the Tonya Harding trial, hoping against hope they'd let her off, let her skate around again. And when in fourth grade I found pot plants growing in Curtis's closet, I watered them with ammonia so he wouldn't be found out.

There was a rumor that Mr.— had dated a former student shortly after she graduated. I don't know if that's true, but Curtis was convinced. One day, Mr.— came into the restaurant where Curtis was working after high school and said something snide like, "No college, huh? You still working in the kitchen?"

Curtis shot back, "You still diddlin' teenage girls?"

I was proud of him for that. My brother, fearless moral defender. My brother, who cared not one lick for what anyone thought.

Of course, he did care what people thought. Some, anyway. His girlfriends, our mom, maybe me. Maybe my dad, although they didn't talk anymore. Perhaps his dad, too, who I didn't even know existed until fifth grade when I unearthed Curtis's baby book and found an unfamiliar name under "father." We were home alone that afternoon, and I remember him emerging from his dank den, long bleach-dipped hair rumpled from a nap. He was looking through the blinds, always looking through the blinds. On our rural road, we could only see trees and the occasional flock of turkeys. I didn't understand what he was always looking for.

"Curt," I said, "Did you know that Dad's, like, not your dad?"

He didn't flinch. He barely blinked.

"Curt," I said.

His eyes followed something I couldn't see beyond the glass.

"Let me know if the mail comes," he said. He hitched up his baggy jeans and shuffled back to his room.

CURTIS ISN'T ALLOWED A PHONE at the recovery center. He's not even allowed to take calls. His only communication with the outside world is through the mail. He fills pages with tiny script on sobriety and gardening and hunting feral hogs and feeling things, really feeling things, all the way down and without relief. How do you people do it? he writes. Feel stuff all the time?

I pace the shag-carpeted length of my apartment while the phone rings. I consider hanging up—he can't even take my call—when a man answers. I begin a rambling speech about how I know residents can't take calls, but that it's my brother's birthday, and I want to know if someone could tell him happy birthday for me. The man says sure, and who should he say called?

"His sister," I say.

"His sister," he says. "Which sister?"

"He only has one," I say, and we hang up.

Days later, I'll remember: we have two stepsisters.

My sense of duty satisfied, I return to my life. I am twenty-six. I am a poet living alone in two cheap rooms with a mountain view. At night, I take bad phone photos of the moon. I don't have a table, and I eat off a plank laid over two chairs. All my friends are beautiful and brilliant and crack me open with laughter at bars, where well liquor is three dollars, and it still feels like there are new kinds of nights to be had.

Still, having thwarted so much of it in youth, trouble isn't quite done with me. Next year, the three-dollar scotch will start bringing on migraines. An old love will be found dead of an overdose, and a hoard of blowflies will descend on my tiny palace from a gap between the built-in pantry and the wall. Some trapped rodent's black-robed soul collectors buzzing and plotting on every summer-bright window. Remember us, they'll say. Or maybe it'll be, Remember us? I'm not sure if I will. If I do. I'm so young, so self-absorbed, the world beyond this fishbowl town a muffled rumor. My brother, who used to fall asleep sitting sentinel in front of my door while our parents argued, is realms away and unsure of the shape his life will take beyond the chores and other troubled men, beyond the ceaseless feeling and confession of feeling, and all I can do is write poems and pursue calamitous relationships and take grainy photos through dirty windows of the moon.

But trouble, now, is done with Curtis. Soon, he'll leave Georgia and start over back home. Over the next ten years, he'll become a master electrician and buy a house and a Dachshund named Squeaks. His son will look exactly like him, eyes aquarium blue. When he reaches for his father's hand, my nephew will find it. My brother's son will know him.

IT'S A MYTH, YOU KNOW, the thing about the goldfish's memory. Goldfish can learn different faces, and if you feed them, they'll take to following you the length of the tank, back and forth, watching through the glass, waiting to be fed or recognized. So many who look just want to be seen. Sometimes, the goldfish will even swim up and take it—take it right out of your hand.

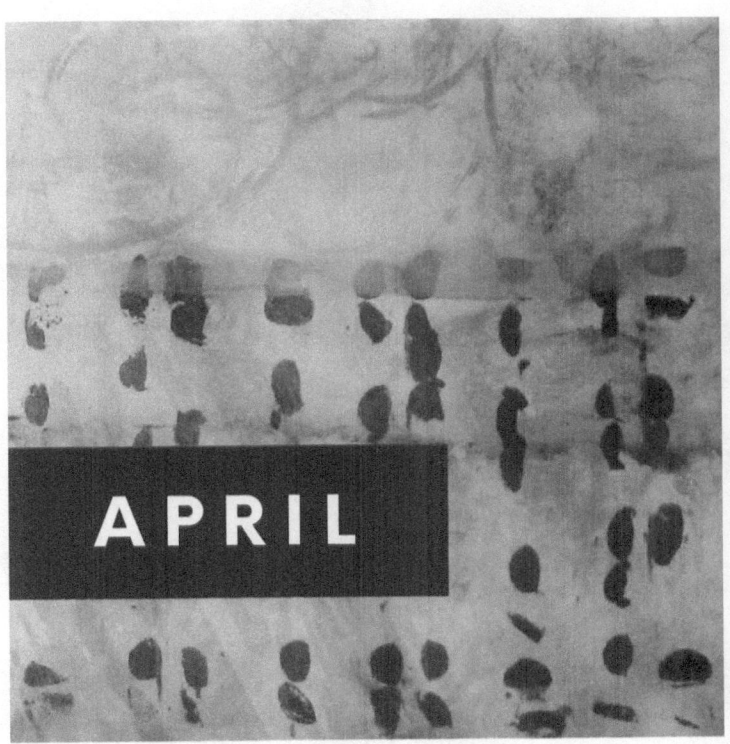

APRIL

"CAN'T I JUST TRY AND ENJOY THE MOMENT?"

Stephen Furlong

April 1

It's a Thursday. A holiday that celebrates pranks and comic mischief. I don't have anything elaborate planned. I'm probably looking forward to the weekend so I can hang out with my best friend. I'm also preparing for the school play, *Dracula*, and I play Hennessey. My character is described as earnest, trim, hardworking, and pleasant. I have the first line.

Miss Seward! What is it?

I AM A SENIOR IN HIGH SCHOOL—a private, all-male, military, college-preparatory, and religious institution. I am probably re-reading *Nineteen Minutes* by Jodi Picoult. I am no longer listening to *Ten*, the debut album of Pearl Jam, every night when I can't sleep. I have switched to a German darkwave group named Diary of Dreams that I found by accident because I was looking up the term Nigredo, which is an album of theirs. Considering alchemy, Nigredo is the Blackness, and is often considered the initial movement toward the philosopher's stone.

MY BIRTHDAY IS IN ELEVEN DAYS, and I don't want any gifts. Just presence.

I am preparing myself mentally for graduation, and I am also battling with myself over a decision I made a couple days prior. I haven't heard back from my top choice and rather than risk potential rejection, I reject them and resign myself to my second choice. The second choice is just that—my second choice. Still, I think my father secretly wishes I'd go there because, even though I'm still a couple hours from home, I'll only be 314 miles away.

Not 1,184 miles away.

I try to calculate those miles in emotional distance.

That becomes what I concern myself with in math class.

I also recognize I would be 1,052 miles away from my best friend.

I try not to think about that. But, you know what happens when you try to avoid something?

It surfaces anyway. I learned that from grief.

I AM SEEING A THERAPIST who is telling me that I'm one of the strongest people he's ever met.

I am resisting the urge to call *bullshit*.

A couple months before he gifts me a movie—a coming-of-age story of an artist struggling in a chaotic household.

He says, *I see parallels. I hope this helps.*

Parallels. Another thing that will probably keep me up at night. And it's not even math related. But I know, and you should know, sleep is not my friend. Hasn't been for some time.

The movie tracks a summer that changed a young artist and his family. The father figure, played by Ray Liotta, is concerned his son doesn't like girls. Believes this artist business is a fad, a phase. The mother figure, played by Diana Scarwid, is aloof, but (I believe) has good intentions. Their son, played by Trevor Morgan, the kid from *Jurassic Park III*, reminds me of myself. He's always afraid he's bothering someone else. Often apologizing for his existence. The mentor in the film, a Russian painter named Serov, played by Armin Mueller-Stahl, often calls him a little shit. Usually lovingly.

The movie is about finding (and holding onto) the beauty in this life, despite the presence of ugliness. When I watched it for the first time, I cried like a baby. And I am okay with that. At least trying to be. Because I am trying to embrace my emotions. But I feel our relationship is like a child chasing their shadow. I'm always a step behind.

The movie is *Local Color*, directed by George Gallo, released in 2006.

MY FATHER WANTS ME to start applying for jobs. I tell him I have enough on my plate. It becomes another fight. I know he means well. But I graduate in six weeks. Can't I just try and enjoy the moment? I heard a teacher say these are the best days of your life.

I resist the urge to say out loud: If that's the case, what a lousy life!

I WONDER IF PEACE is an option.

"THERE WAS A BOY"

Brandon Taylor

On April 5th of that year, I was anxious and hot and sweating all the time. That was the year of AP exams and graduation and whatever hazy world lurked in the near future. That was a Thursday, and so I was likely sitting in AP English Literature or AP Calculus, trying desperately not to fall asleep. I was in love with a boy who was tall and blond and hopelessly heterosexual. I was in love with my best friend. The air was thick except when it was stirred by a breeze that also swirled the kudzu leaves.

I was watching my friends get ready to go to college and thinking that I myself had no particular post-graduation plans. My stomach hurt almost every day because I was both trying to starve myself into a beautiful, lean shape and also because every time I thought of graduation, I also thought of having to take the ACT and AP exams and also how those two things seemed pointless because I wasn't also working on college applications. It seemed like such an impossible thing to broach with my parents, and yet my teachers kept wanting to know where they should send my letters of recommendation. I was silent on both fronts, which only made the pain in my stomach worse.

My cousin's birthday is April 3rd, so I was probably thinking about going home and pinching off some of the cake still at my grandmother's house. I almost certainly was still thinking about the growing distance between my cousin and me, the way we had started out one way and now stood on the brink of divergent lives. There was a time when our mothers dressed us like twins. There was a time when I was taller than he was. But ten years ago, he was not only taller but more muscular. Football had transformed him, rendered all the softness of his boyish body into something tougher, meaner. I had grown softer and rounder, my manners going shy and turning inward. So, certainly, I was probably thinking about how we had changed and become not merely different versions of ourselves, but different people entirely.

There was a boy I was having sex with, but I was not in love with him. I was probably also thinking about sucking him off in the narrow trailer in the woods and of the way birds' shadows sometimes fell across his stomach while I was down there between his legs. It would not have been unusual for me to have been counting the minutes down by feeling my desire swell inside of me, like a thirst or a changing mood slowly taking hold. I didn't particularly like him, and besides, he was also fucking a girl whose father had raped me, so I had my reasons for keeping things between us cool.

I don't have a particularly strong recollection of this day, but I do know which forces were acting upon it at the time. I know that in April, Alabama is a deep, green sea. The leaves are often damp with fresh rainfall, which comes as a pale, gray mist or a slate torrent. In April, my grandfather had root vegetables out on a table on his back porch, and my grandmother cooked with the back door propped open. There was flour in the air, the scent of black pepper and salt. The heat was slow and heavy, like honey spread over the world.

On April evenings, it is possible to watch birds in the cool, blue dusk flit back and forth over the road.

"I AM STRUCK BY HOW UPBEAT I SOUND"

Heather Gudenkauf

Ten years ago, on April 10th, I was working as an Instructional Coach at my local school district, preparing for the release of my first novel and spending typical family time with my husband and three kids.

That spring, my thirteen-year-old son had been complaining of some pain in his leg. I was convinced that it was growing pains—after all, he had shot up to nearly six feet tall in a short amount of time and was very active. "Take an aspirin," I said. Still, the swelling and pain continued, and I took Alex to the doctor.

"This isn't good," the doctor said after taking X-rays. "This isn't good at all." He placed the X-ray on the lightboard and even to my non-medical eye I could see there was a large mass just above his left knee.

Within days, Alex was admitted to the University of Iowa Children's Hospital, had a biopsy, a port implanted, and began chemotherapy for bone cancer.

I sent an email update to friends and family the week of April 12th:

Everyone—

Alex is still in Iowa City as of this evening (going on 2 weeks now). His counts are good and his fevers are down, but he's been in quite a bit of pain and his leg seems to be more swollen. Because of this, the doctors decided to do another MRI on Friday night and we learned today that while parts of the tumor are dying it seems to be growing also. We will find out tomorrow if Alex will be able to come home or if they will start his second round of chemo right away. I have mixed feelings on this—I think it will do him a world of good to be in his own bed for a few days, but I also want to get going with the chemo and let it do its job!

Alex continues to amaze us—we are so proud of his strength. Despite the pain, boredom and ever-changing discharge dates he is hanging in there. The doctors gave Alex a pass to get out of the hospital for a few hours, so he and Scott were able to go out for lunch today.

Thank you for all the prayers and positive thoughts being sent our way. The support that everyone is giving us reminds us of the beautiful blessings that can come in the midst of a very terrible thing.

Yours,
Heather

When I reread the email, I am struck by how upbeat I sound when really I was absolutely terrified. Fortunately, we had an amazing support system of family and friends who were there for us every single step of the way. My husband was a rock and whenever I felt like I was going to give everything over to fear, I'd look to him and the world would seem to right itself a bit.

During the nine months of treatment, Alex had dozens of inpatient visits, plummeting white blood cell counts, numerous fevers, a blood clot, a faulty port that needed to be replaced, blood transfusions, and had his leg amputated. He had to learn how to walk again and to face a new reality as a cancer survivor and amputee.

As a family, we learned to navigate a new normal. Cancer impacts the entire family and the siblings of those with cancer have a unique set of challenges. For me I was scared, heartbroken and so grateful for the top-notch healthcare my son received from world-class doctors and nurses at The University of Iowa Children's Hospital.

Ten years later, Alex is cancer free, a college-graduate and one of the bravest people I know. His sisters have grown into compassionate, strong young women. We are so proud of them all. And today, more than ever, those final words of that ten-year-old email still rings true: beautiful blessings can come in the midst of a very terrible thing.

"PATIENCE, LIZA; YOU'LL GET THERE."

Liza Olson

I have a different name, different face, different body. I don't yet know that my obsession with the way people can and do change will be taken to a surprising yet completely traceable and satisfying conclusion. I am still in a relationship I will have long since left ten years later, finishing up a screenwriting major I won't pursue in a state I'll only return to after some much-needed time away. I'm still a couple years out from breaking off the engagement, moving across the country, and quitting my job.

Today, April 13th, I'm only three days away from screening early footage of the short film I wrote. A producing student picked the project: a story about a trans girl and her becoming. I didn't know then why I connected so strongly to the premise but, ten years later, figured it all out.

Most days, I'm operating under a high level of repression, shoving questioning thoughts down with work, putting everything I have into screenwriting and, somewhere below the conscious level, telling myself that if I can't be the person I want to be, I can at least be known for something. At least put together words that might live on. My life, as it has since puberty, feels like a ticking time bomb. The constant hum-buzz of dread and anxiety—which I attribute to depression but is actually more gender dysphoria—is an ever-present driver of my emotional state. It will largely disappear in ten years' time, within a week of starting hormone replacement therapy.

Re-reading journal entries from this time period makes me physically cringe now. How hard I tried to make things work that were never going to. Tried to fit a mold I was never going to fit, a mold that wasn't meant for me (if it's meant for anyone). I lived my life in a way that would make the people around me happy without ever considering what would make *me* happy. It would come out in ways that frustrated me: over-eating and drinking till sickness, then counting every calorie, running till I nearly passed out, weighing myself several times a day. I'd self-correct when it got too serious, address the problem, but it was always the management of symptoms—never the cause.

I look to others like someone who knows what they want and goes after it. I lose the weight, run the races, write the scripts, and win the prizes, but the truth I can't or won't share is that any other first step is easier for me than this one is, that transition is the upheaval I need but am afraid of right now, that in the hyper-masculine environment I grew up in, going along to get along was what I chose, so I competed in the wrestling tournaments, slapped on the helmet and pads come fall, scrapped and fought over silly things in my old neighborhood—anything to maintain the illusion.

I will come to appreciate the eventual breakdown in time, its cascading, butterfly effect changes that got me where I needed to be. It'll start with walking away from screenwriting in my final semester despite being the department wunderkind and returning to my first love, fiction, instead. It'll continue with writing the things I want, getting started in publishing, and beginning the novel that will force me, finally, to look inward. As I start to see myself more clearly, I'll also see the codependent cracks in the relationship I'm in, realize that I don't even want this, I'm not happy, I feel trapped. Today, though, April 13th, the book is just the germ of an idea kicking around the back of my mind.

I'll break off the engagement while I'm in the hospital, barely make it through the next couple of months, nearly die and go to the hospital again, then get away for good. I'll turn to that first love to get through the months that follow, writing my way out as the germ of a new idea forms in the back of my mind: I think I might be trans.

I will make new friends, form connections, develop as a writer, and explore the queer identity I'd buried so deep for so long. I will learn more about myself in a year than I had in the preceding twenty-five. I'll learn to value myself, identify and dismantle negative self-talk. All the ways I used to hurt myself will fall away without my having to consciously address them anymore. I will find my way back to myself and, in time, meet the person who will love me for me.

Ten years later, and I've come out as trans, changed my name. I've been on HRT for nearly a year now, my face and body already different, making me look like the sister of my former self. Early on in my transition, I'll occasionally get caught up in thoughts like, *This would've been easier if you'd done it years ago*, and *It would've saved you a lot of hurt*. But the truth is I didn't have the awareness, experience, fortitude I have now, which I needed every bit of in the early stages.

Re-reading the short script I wrote ten years ago brings happy tears now. How easy it was for me to relate to that trans girl, how natural it felt to write from that perspective. And of course, the fact that, without even realizing it, I'd picked a name for myself that was only a letter off from hers. On April 13th, I was on the cusp: waiting for a screening, for graduation, for freedom, for becoming. It's ten years later, and if I could I'd go back, give myself a hug, answer her inevitable questions, and tell her, "Patience, Liza. You'll get there."

"WHAT ARE YOU HUNGRY FOR?"

Amanda Futrell

April 15

I was sitting in a hospital in a room full of women, all of us determined to starve to death. I was asked to write down three things I was grateful for. Number one was my best friend Katy, with whom I spent most of my early adulthood joined at the hip and was like a sister to me. Number two, my grandfather who was like a father. And number three, my husband. Within a decade, none of these people would be in my life. My grandfather would soon die at the age of ninety-two. In four years, Katy would lose her fight with congenital heart disease at the age of thirty-five, making me even more eager to have a daughter named after her. That was when my ex-husband changed his mind about children, which was another way of saying he changed his mind about me.

That day, I didn't starve, or do one thousand sit-ups, or smoke cigarettes. Instead, I spent hours googling exotic strains of weed. I chewed Nicorette until my gums bled. I ducked into a dark bar at 11:45 in the morning on a Thursday, telling no one I was there. The bartender was a young, finely chiseled thing preparing a gin and fresh grapefruit juice with her back turned to me. The cursive tattoo between her brittle-looking shoulder blades read, *The seasons have changed and so have I.*

I wish I could say the same. It's true, I no longer starve, but, as a result, I have to eat through the raw emotions, feeling everything that made me desperate enough to whittle myself down to nothing. Added to that is a new complaint that's been front and center since Katy's death—a profound, unending loneliness that follows me into crowds. Over and over again, during rehab, we, the starving ladies, were asked, What are you hungry for? What are you starving away? It was a question I knew the answer to but didn't dare speak out loud because frankly, my own neediness sickened me. I was starving for connection, intimacy, excitement, love, a family, and more. Today, I can't help but ask myself, if I couldn't feel fulfilled when the three most supportive people in my life were in my corner, what chance do I have now?

Ten years have passed, and I still don't know how to live with my seemingly never-ending needs. Instead, I try to spend as much time as possible ignoring them. How I do that most these days is play pinball. I play so damned much that the man behind the counter never asks for my membership card. Johnny-Behind-the-Counter is California mellow, Midwest genuine and sometimes gently calls me "Champ." He once told me it makes him laugh every time a new player says, "The ball went right down the middle."

"That's exactly what a pinball machine is designed to do," he says. To drain, to go "right down the middle."

Today, the pinball machine is doing exactly what it is designed to do. A bumper sends the ball pinging wildly towards the outlying lane. At the last second, the ball grazes a post and begins bouncing back and forth, back and forth—the most dangerous motion in pinball. I nudge the machine, but the hazardous pinging continues. The ball is nowhere near the flippers, yet, I know it will drain if I don't do something. And, still, I've done everything I know to do.

In desperation, I clamp both hands on each side and yank downward—the Death Save— which does absolutely nothing to alter the ball's side to side motion. All I can hope is that soon, some unknown instinct I have will float to the surface—that today I won't drain, simply because I don't want to.

"CHANGE HAD BEEN SET IN MOTION LONG AGO"

Joel Coltharp

April 22

B ack then, Saturday nights were for sacred rituals: the four of us, the last of our kind, standing on Randy's back porch, cold beers in hand, telling war stories that we'd all heard a hundred times before—a running competition to see who'd had it worse, measured in missed meals, getting the belt, and lame sex. We'd watch bad movies in Randy's unfinished basement until we were good and drunk and then white-knuckle the drive home, back to Mark's dingy apartment and Andrew's broken marriage and my sleeping wife and son, back through the only city we'd ever known.

Once, there had been more of us. Once, we had done this every night, hiding out at each other's apartments as soon as we were free of the second shift, only surrendering to the sameness of the next day as dawn broke, but too much had already been lost to day jobs and unexpected offspring and beckoning girl-friends. So now, we held on with both hands to the only thing reminding us of what we'd always been. It didn't matter that Randy had been laid off again or that Mark and Andrew's father was back in the hospital, dying of cancer this time—Saturday nights were mandatory.

Once, I'd been as devout as the rest of them, and every Sat-urday night I'd return to the north side I'd abandoned years before, feeling my jaw harden as subdivisions and office parks morphed into those same old scrap yards and flea markets. I kept my head on a swivel while buying beer at the liquor store around the corner from Randy's house—just down the street from where I'd grown up—recalling that clinched feeling I used to always carry in my gut as a kid. Wedged my car into Randy's driveway while avoiding all the ones he and his father kept around that didn't run. Listening to the oddly comforting refrain of the neighbors arguing over who used up the last of their meth, while the junkyard dog one yard over begged for them to stop.

Lately, though, I'd started missing a few Saturdays here and there. Lately, I'd been dodging questions the rest of the week about where the hell I'd been. And lately, Saturday nights had become about hiding a shameful secret: I'd gone back to school, a move made on a whim when faced with yet another job disappearing out from under me, yet another chance to start over at the bottom of the ladder. I'd just been messing around at first, seeing how the other three-quarters lived, but then one class had led to another, and before I knew it, I had a major and a bunch of clean-scrubbed classmates who were beginning to recognize my face.

Worst of all, I'd decided to enroll full-time. To make a run at something that had always seemed off-limits. I'd been at it for three years, and the time had come to jump in or get out. But that meant blowing up the whole thing into something that could no longer be hidden, and I'd been putting off breaking the news for as long as I could.

Come April, I still hadn't said a word, had missed a few Saturdays in a row to make sure I didn't, and when I finally dragged myself back over to Randy's house, I felt like I'd been gone for years. The others were already on their second six-packs, and Randy was bumming cigarettes off those of us still collecting paychecks. Mark was in one of his dark moods, drowning his sorrows in Bud Light and tossing out the usual complaints about this new girl he'd been seeing like he was bare-handing bottle rockets, while Andrew detailed the latest diagnosis: their mother had spots on her lungs. Andrew was chain-smoking

Marlboro Reds like I hadn't seen him do since our barfly days. Randy was walking around shirtless, talking up his plans to start tracking down the girls he'd missed out on back in high school and staggering around the corner of the house to piss against the foundation like he was punishing it for being so run-down.

The nearby train tracks sprang to life with a long line of freight cars, and I thought about how I'd been listening to that same train my entire life, and about the look on the other guys' faces when I told them I was getting married, becoming the first to take the plunge, all those years ago. They'd looked at me then like I'd broken some kind of vow, and I realized that whatever was about to change had been set in motion long ago.

THESE DAYS, SATURDAY NIGHTS are for squinting at my laptop screen, trying to make out Randy and Andrew's drunken audio. We watch bad movies through pirated software until we run out of things to say, then we log off and return to our separate lives. Sometimes, we think to email throughout the week, but mostly we leave each other be.

These days, Randy doesn't bother looking for work, but he gets out more than the rest of us, helping his father make the rounds to all his rental properties on the north side. Andrew frets about his hours getting cut, but at least he finally got around to pulling the plug on his marriage and rented a little place over by our old high school to be close to his kids before everything changed. And we don't hear from Mark anymore: he married that same girl and then quit us altogether, but not before drinking himself into the hospital.

I still go to bed each Saturday night feeling guilty: I've lucked into a teaching job at the local university, making more money than my parents ever made together, and I spend my days squinting at my laptop screen, seeing a bunch of clean-scrubbed faces staring back at me. They do a good job acting like they want to hear what I have to say, but I feel certain, whenever I catch one of them giving me an odd look, that they can see all those old Saturday nights all over me.

"I WAS SHARING A HOUSE WITH A GHOST"

Lacey Rowland

May 5th was the last week before finals, and I was sitting in my American Literature survey class in the Liberal Arts building on campus. The classroom had a distinct mugginess in the afternoon from being air-conditioned by a swamp cooler that rattled in the ceiling. It's one of those buildings that never got updated because it houses departments that are small and insignificant. The instructor was an older woman who constantly talked about golf and only assigned the male authors from the anthology. In May, in the afternoon, Boise takes on a pinkish hue and lights up the nearby foothills. Magnolia blooms turn from clenched fists to open palms. Cottonwoods shed their down and the Boise River cuts slow and low along the campus. It's hard to sit still when the world wakes up.

I was engaged to a man who was thirteen years my senior. He was a widower. That was his most defining attribute. I was just twenty-three years old then and planning my wedding in between potty training my fiancé's twin toddlers and writing essays about the Beats and Modernism. That week I would've been laid off from my seasonal gig at the convenience store on campus and transitioning to taking care of the kids full time. On May 5th, I was savoring the fleeting independence of intermittent childlessness. I could still pocket my ring and pretend I was alone.

That spring, I became an amateur archaeologist. I was sharing a house with a ghost. In the bathroom under the sink, there was a box of expired pregnancy tests and lemon-scented perfume. In the basement, boxes of knick-knacks, old scarves and blouses, diaries, textbooks, and her Weight Watchers binder. The late wife had been a reader too, in love with literature like I was. My fiancé didn't talk about her much. What I learned about her, I found through my own snooping when he was away and the twins were napping. Sometimes I'd spend hours sifting through her things in the basement trying to learn about a woman I would always be compared to but never meet. Who was this person who saved crafting moss in a Tupperware container and wore slinky, black leather boots?

I found an old cell phone that belonged to my fiancé in a cupboard and played the last voicemail she'd left for him. It was something about groceries, something inconsequential, like all voicemails are when you're happily married and unaware that you'll drop dead in a few weeks from a pulmonary embolism. Her voice had a higher pitch than I'd imagined. It was tragic. She was so young. That's what they said about her anyway. I remember resisting the urge to delete the message and erase a part of her.

In the classroom, trying to pay attention to the lecture on Hemingway or Jack London, my thoughts were drifting to her. She was a constant shadow I couldn't shake. I wondered if she was a better student than me. A better mother. A better lover. At night when my fiancé and I would have sex, I feared he would cry her name as he came. I tried not to see the similarities in our appearance. We both had short, dark hair and fair skin. You could describe us as sturdy women. I ended up getting highlights in my hair and exercised obsessively to keep trim.

I was checking boxes in May. Finishing classes. Buying a wedding dress. Pleasing my parents. Fulfilling God's will. Settling down. Playing the dutiful mother. Cleaning house. Planning the wedding, but not what comes after.

When class finished, the chairs screeched along the tile floor as we made our way out into the fleeting afternoon sun.

I savored those afternoons, between school or work and the half-mile walk to the daycare to pick up the twins. Some days I took the long way along the river. Some days I walked through the neighborhood where I used to live on Potter Street in the one-bedroom basement apartment. I'd pass the community garden, which was mostly weeds, and the Mormon church, until I got to Beacon Street and the pink stucco daycare center.

These days I can no longer hear the late wife's voice with much clarity. The twins have a new stepmother. I'm at another precipice in my life now. My partner and I have been discussing the future, though I'm more cautious. We fantasize about buying a home, having children together. But for now, we're content to be as we are—happily cohabitating in our little apartment with two cats and no ghosts. In the yard, our magnolia tree is getting ready to bloom.

"A POP ANTHEM FOR THE
GREAT PLAGUE"

Refael Paul Arenson

May 6

The pilot's voice boomed, crackling over the PA. "Ladies and gentlemen, can't believe what I'm hearing. We're going back to the terminal."

I looked up, startled. My Rome to London flight sat on the Fiumicino runway. Through the cabin window, I saw the deep green canopy of Mediterranean pines beyond the tarmac, blue sea glinting.

The Icelandic volcano Eyjafjallajökull was belching a plume of fine ash into the polar jet stream, to a height of nine kilometers—the cruising altitude of large aircraft. The ash, sucked into jet turbines, fused to liquid glass that ground moving blades, blocked valves, choked engines. Air traffic around Europe screeched to a halt.

Trip canceled. I was lucky, I could go home. Other passengers? Not so lucky.

The internet fed us news. Air routes closed and opened unpredictably as the ash cloud drifted, dissipated, reemerged. No-fly zones shifted from day to day, week to week—amorphous black blobs on maps, tentacles streaming over the Northern Hemisphere. The ash bled west past Prince Edward Island in Canada, and east over Siberia, almost to Lake Baikal.

Amidst panic, rental cars evaporated. Trains booked out for weeks ahead. Taxi drivers earned thousands of euros for rides to Paris, Brussels, Berlin.

Air traffic was interrupted for ten weeks. Twenty countries closed their airspace. A hundred thousand flights were canceled. Ten million passengers were stranded, in Europe and around the world—the largest air shutdown since WWII. Until now.

TEN YEARS LATER, I left Rome.

The plane approached Bangkok—a whited-out sky, dingy pink mist. As we floated lower, small spots of water glistened below, just visible through the haze.

"Perché vai in Thailandia?" my friends had asked me. *"Sei matto?"* Are you mad?

The news was coming from China. A mysterious illness. People collapsing in the streets, gasping like fish. Wuhan built two hospitals overnight. Chinese New Year was canceled.

No sooner had I left Italy, Lombardia and Veneto declared quarantine zones. The irony.

Then all of Italy was in quarantine. All of Europe. The Philippines, India, Vietnam. California, New York, and where next? Don't go to work. Don't go to school. Don't leave home.

In Bergamo, in Brescia, in Brooklyn and Detroit, there was nowhere to put the bodies. They went into refrigerator trucks.

I SAT IN BANGKOK, glued to the internet. New words and phrases flung about. Coronavirus. Lockdown. Social distancing. Shelter in place. Self-quarantine. Auto-declaration. Covid. Pandemic.

Or should that be pandemonium?

International borders closed. Australia, Canada, New Zealand called citizens home. Flights were scrubbed, as during the volcano ten years earlier.

Stranded foreigners mobbed immigration offices until blanket visas were granted. Thais watch their livelihoods vanish, oblique desperation in their eyes.

We washed our hands until chapped skin split our knuckles. Our temperature was taken in public, infrared thermometers aimed at our foreheads like revolvers. What would happen if we measured over 37.5 degrees Celsius? We didn't ask.

The alcohol ban came next.

No news of my return flight that was scheduled the following Monday. The airline office was closed. No one answered the phones. I filled out web forms, received polite emails promising a reply in four to six weeks. I tracked down Twitter accounts, wrote DMs. More careful, noncommittal messages.

Desperate for news, I braved the airport train, eerily deserted, to Suvarnabhumi Airport. On the screen of scheduled departures, for every ten flights, eight were canceled. Check-in was open for London, Nanning, Ko Samui, and two flights to Shanghai.

Was my carrier flying? No.

A squad of doctors sat in the departure hall. White hazmat coveralls, black goggles, blue latex gloves. They sat in lounge chairs, trolley suitcases standing around them. Shocked, I realized—they were not doctors. These were passengers. Early for their flight, waiting to check in.

My airline's ticket office bore a sign: "Temporarily closed for COVID-19."

"SUPER SPREADER," the latest luk thung pop song, was the hot new comeback for Thai singing stars Jane, Noon and Bow. They'd revived their 2010 hit "Super Valentine" for the Covid era. Decked in black high heels, black jeans, clear plastic face visors, they bopped and swayed one meter apart. Social distancing.

Supah sa-pread-euh!
Supah sa-pread-euh!
Co-vid jeu chua rao ja suay thuk khon!

Each word split in syllables, perfect cadence of Thai tones, female particle *"ka."* A bouncy beat belied Grim Reaper lyrics.

Superspreader! Superspreader! If Covid finds us, we're all out of luck.

Covid, ka. Covid, ka. My name's Co, I come with Fever and Cough.

Cough cough cough! Sneeze sneeze sneeze! If you can't recover, you could die!

*People had to be carted away. If you want to live, stay in your homes.**

Thai people love to have fun, and there it was, a pop anthem for the Great Plague. The unreal becoming every day. Our lives were changing.

In springtime, Rome's a riot of wisteria with thick masses of purple flowers swaying from monuments, sweet perfume drifting. But that year I wouldn't see it. I might never see it again. What was the future of air travel? In the new era, would we still buy tickets online, hop on planes wherever we want? Would it be so easy?

In Bangkok, gritty concrete blocks piled the horizon, blurred in smoggy air. Golden temples glinted where sunlight struck them. In Lumphini Park, rain trees with hemispherical crowns, studded with pink brush blooms, lined the walkways. Flame trees with fiery orange sprays, cascaded in sheaves. Frangipane trees thick with fleshy white flowers, fragrant as gardenias.

*Read full lyrics at Khaosod English: https://www.khaosod english.com/life/2020/04/14/govt-recruits-meme-superstars-jane-noon-bow-for-its-covid-19-song/

"THE BUNKER"

Jon Hickey

Ten years ago on May 10th, I was living in a basement apartment on Blair Street, just down the hill from College-town. It was only half underground, with windows and a porch that overlooked the corner of Blair and Cook. This basement apartment was the setting for many self-created crises and bad scenes, but also some good parties and late-night recording sessions. My friends and I called the apartment "The Bunker," a safe place to hide from the drudgery and realities of writing and teaching and our other responsibilities as decent human beings.

The floor was a snake pit of cables. We had all the instruments: a Fender Telecaster and a Deluxe Reverb amplifier, a Squier P-Bass, a Pearl travel drum kit on the raised kitchenette floor. We banged out music and recorded covers and original songs on a digital 8-track recorder. Sometimes we managed to sound good, although the evidence of this competence is sparse. Friends would drop by to ostensibly work on tracks, but we'd usually manage to have a drink and a smoke, and little actual work got done.

What I remember about that time is a feeling of transience and uncertainty. I had finished my MFA at Cornell, and I still had a year left of my lectureship, but my cohort and I could see the end of our time in Ithaca. I'd applied to fellowships and had fallen flat on my face, as I would a year later. I was desperate for a gig teaching comp, desperate to pay the rent for The Bunker and the bills for the credit cards I was living on (and would spend the better part of a decade paying off). On May 10th, final grades for the semester were submitted to the English office, student emails demanding changes to them were arriving and ignored, and my friends and I were preparing to drift off to our corners of the world for the summer. I would see some of my friends when we returned in the fall, but others I would never see again. We'd successfully delayed our entry into the great terrifying world, but it was knocking at the door of The Bunker.

A new professor on campus used to hang out with us lecturers. Sometimes he would bring a six-pack of Yuengling to my porch, and we would listen to the Stones and the Beatles and we would watch the undergrads pass by on Blair Street. He was going through a painful divorce, and he hated being stuck in this town upstate. This professor had written a book that had received a good amount of acclaim, and in our long afternoons on the porch, it became clear that success had failed to solve the significant problems of his life. You will yearn for these days, this professor would say. I do not. That year was the beginning of an unpleasant process of reorienting my expectations and dreams, a massive correction, and I'm glad I'm on the other side of it.

I live in San Francisco with my wife and son. We live in our own place two floors above the basement. It's been a long time since I've had a drink and a long time since I've smoked anything. Every morning I wake up to my son calling out to me from his crib, my wife getting ready for another day in clinic. Sometimes when I'm watching my son in the afternoon, I'll pick up my acoustic guitar and strum out a few chords of a half-remembered song from those days in The Bunker. My son will reach out for the strings and strum his own rhythm. The path here ridicules the elaborate plans and illusions I had when I was twenty-six years old. Today I live not for my ambitions, but to be the person who deserves this happy life.

"A PARTNER WHO SIMPLY LETS ME BE"

Chital Mehta

It's May 12th, a hot summer day in Chennai. I feel the sweat soaking my salwar. I have lived in this city for four years, but I still haven't gotten used to the heat. Each summer, the heat-wave feels like a rude surprise, although it comes with the same intensity. I drink from my water bottle, but the water doesn't make it to my belly. It feels as if the sun soaks the water before it can wet my mouth. My parents have recently spoken with my boyfriend's parents about a possible marriage. His mother came from a superstitious family and was convinced that I was an outsider born to break the family apart.

I feel broken after my parents tell me that the answer is negative. After work, I walk to a nearby temple, even though I'm not religious. I go because my boyfriend's mother is a deeply religious person. I walk inside and take in the smell of camphor and sandalwood mixed with the fragrance of jasmine flowers. It's a holy place but does nothing to comfort the storm inside my heart.

But I whisper to the statue of Hanuman, and all other gods to whom she prayed every day, to somehow make this work; to somehow pave the path for my marriage to this person who I believe is good for me.

A marriage does happen a few months later after a prolonged wait and countless conversations. I don't think much about what kind of life I am looking forward to. I don't think much about what writing will mean to me in a few years. I only know I have to somehow materialize my two-year relationship into marriage.

I still do not believe in idol worship. My mother-in-law has been waking up at four a.m. for years now to light a lamp and pray. She will wash each silver lamp meticulously and decorate them with wet vermilion. She will fill the lamps with ghee and light a wick. This takes at least two hours of her day. While I don't believe that praying to a statue brings any difference, I have developed a newfound respect for her devotion.

It's been ten years and I know it wasn't a wrong move. I only listened to what my heart inclined toward, to marry the person I loved. And it wasn't just about love, I realize now. It was also more about what I wanted from life. A couple of years after the wedding, I decided to write, to take a path that is filled with rejections and failures. I am struggling to fill a blank page each morning, but what comforts me is having a partner who simply lets me be.

"IN THE END, WE WERE DEEMED AN IRREFUTABLE MATCH"

Sage Ravenwood

May 30

I truly believe Pickles survived Hurricane Katrina, heartworms, and an endless shuffle of shelters so she could save me. In some weird context, it made sense that both of us, having suffered, would choose the other. I didn't feel worthy. There are only so many ways you can stay broken, suicidal, and stuck in an endless loop of therapy. My sudden deafness had left me locked inside my head with every single trauma possible.

Little did I know, soon my life would no longer be up for debate. Not if a dog had anything to say about it.

Trained as a working dog for the deaf, Pickles arrived from International Hearing Dog, Inc. on December 12th. I never thought of renaming her for a second. She was my personality in dog form with a *pickled* attitude. That first week of being leashed together 24/7 felt more like punishment than training to our *"conjoined impatient souls."* In the end, we were deemed an irrefutable match.

Two weeks after her arrival, I ended up with a severe lung infection. I woke up to Pickles' head beside mine on the pillow with bloodshot eyes, her body upright leaning on the bed. She had stayed awake all night watching over me. I knew then, I would never be able to repay a love like that. How does anyone repay a love like that?

To this day, I tell people my greatest teacher was a dog. Stubborn as all get out, she would sit, refusing to budge until I slowed down to notice the world around us. This is how she taught me to hear with my eyes, redirecting my attention to things like a woodpecker drilling a pine tree, children squealing playfully, or car tires on gravel. Watch the movement to see what you can't hear was her dog motto. Whenever she saw that I got it, her face lit up like it was the greatest thing to happen to her.

It was amusing when people didn't know my name, but readily knew hers. You couldn't bottle her personality. In a Barnes & Noble bookstore she always pretended to faint, laying on her side in the aisle, one eye open, chuckling to see if I noticed. People stared at us bewildered by the deaf woman and her manic-looking dog laughing it up. She had this impossible-to-ignore crazy-ass grin. She would stick her head under bathroom stalls to say hi to people, we would rush out with shrieks following our exit. If any of those women ever read this, we sincerely apologize.

Surviving Katrina left Pickles with her own fears of rain and horses. I never minded waiting in cars or stores, under the bed with her until she felt safe. Training or not, her needs were just as important as mine. If not more. In turn, she was my ears and heart. Where one ended the other began. Human and dog melded in synchronicity.

Pickles died of Acute Leukemia on May 30th. She was only seven years old; I was fortunate to be her human for six of those years. That day, without warning, she collapsed in the tall grass, blood pouring from her nose. There wasn't enough time to say goodbye. There are days I still look for her when it rains. On those days when the silence becomes too much I find a way through—not for me, mind you—for a dog who would be mighty pissed off if she saw me before my time.

Ten years later, the pain remains as raw as the day I lost her. I still can't find words or eloquence worthy enough to remember her by. Perhaps because she never truly left, and I never let go.

Time doesn't replace what's missing. I still struggle to navigate my deafness; I rescue now. So many animals have come and gone. Today, there are two dogs in my home (Bjarki and Yazhi), along with a one-eyed cat (Max), plus two more cats (Shua and Vinny). On some level, it feels right to save as many of these abandoned animals as I can—the same way Pickles and I saved one another. We broke all the right rules in the best possible way. Every single day for the rest of my life, I will continue to miss my sidekick.

"I'M SO PROUD OF YOU, YOU BEAUTIFUL IDIOT!"

Kathryn Caves

Ten years ago, I thought I knew who I was. I gave every appearance of knowing myself—who I was, what I wanted, where I was going, why I wanted these things. Scrutinizing my past self simultaneously makes me proud of my determination and cringe at my choices. At age nineteen, I was finding my voice but hadn't fully found it yet. I didn't know what I was capable of. I knew I was capable of people-pleasing, getting straight As, and fitting into the evangelical world. I knew I wanted to be a pharmacist and make my parents happy. It's strange to look back and realize which pieces were me, and which pieces I was trying to shove into a mold meant for an entirely different person.

On May 13th, I was packing up my freshman dorm room, which had been carefully coordinated in a vibrant teal and disgusting lime green. I had done what every promising young writer does: go to the University of Iowa to take every pharmacy school prerequisite and exactly zero creative writing classes. I was so sure of my decision to become a pharmacist that I applied for a doctorate of pharmacy program the next fall. With a year of college under my belt, I was fully committed to going to school to learn how to help doctors NOT KILL PEOPLE. To be fair, by the end of my freshman year, I had accomplished quite a lot. I had clawed my way through the weeded-out chemistry classes and gotten my first non-A final grade. I had participated in a twenty-four-hour dance marathon and broke the rules by taking caffeine-laced Excedrin. I had gone through a shockingly cut-throat interview process to lock down a lucrative resident assistant gig the next semester. Unfortunately, the one thing I hadn't done was take a good, hard look at how my life plan was meant for a Kathryn in an alternate universe. The last ten years of my life have been a huge lesson in the fact that just because you CAN do something, that does not by any means require you to DO something. I would laugh remembering all of the signs that I should never have been a pharmacist, if only it hadn't put me in so much debt. For example, just because you CAN eek your way through organic chemistry and burst into tears during only one exam, does NOT mean you should pursue a STEM field. Just because you CAN tolerate hospital smells does NOT mean you should marry yourself to working in one. Just because you CAN pronounce the drug name levetiracetam without sounding like you're choking does NOT mean you should take out loans to ensure you can say that word often, with an air of authority. Today, with exactly one month left of my twenties, I can't change the decisions I made at 19 or the fact that I paid a sickening amount of money to add PharmD at the end of my name. I can't rid myself of the title "Pharmacist" unless I do something very illegal.

Looking back on May 13th, with exactly one month left of my teens, I'm not sure if my absolute certainty about my life's path makes me want to snort-laugh, sob, or yell, "I'M SO PROUD OF YOU, YOU BEAUTIFUL IDIOT!" I am certain, however, that ten years ago, if someone had told me I'd one day be a writer living in New York City instead of feigning enthusiasm as a pharmacist, I would have done all three at once.

"IT TOOK TEN YEARS TO LEARN THIS LESSON"

Katie Quach

In Mexico City (*Day-effay*, the pet name *everyone* uses for it), I sometimes take the train to work. The walk to the Chupaltapec Metro Station is only three blocks from my ground-floor apartment in *La Condesa*. At the end of my street is a juice stand. At 6:30 in the morning on June 4th, a small group of men gather here. They might be drinking juice or eating cubes of fruit from clear plastic take-away containers. Mostly, they watch and wait for something to happen so they can talk about it. They see me approaching from across the street and grow still. I sense what's about to happen before it does.

"China! China!" they erupt (but it actually sounds like, "CHEEE-NAAA! CHEEE-NAAA!"). They scream this from across the street; their fists pumping in the air in joy, aggression, or both, I can't be sure. I hear clapping, then whistling. I keep walking. How else am I supposed to react? My eyes focus on the ground, looking for constellations among the dark patches of gum stuck to the sidewalk.

Afterward, I reenact the scene for my friends. They laugh at my imitation of the juice stand men. I bug my eyes out. I make myself look like a crazed *fútbol* coach on the sidelines. It makes for a good, self-deprecating story. And wasn't that the point of leaving home two years ago, in search of a good story? I abandoned my family during a crisis to collect stories from abroad. Now that I'm about to return home, I'm not sure sacrificing my family was worth the stories I've collected.

I work as a fourth-grade classroom teacher at an international school in D.F.; my first real teaching job. My students are the light-skinned descendants of Spanish conquistadors. It's rumored a boy in the class next door arrives at school by helicopter, landing on the helipad at the hospital down the street. My students call me "Miss," pronounced *Meees*. I don't think they know my name. They brag about their second, third, fourth homes in Aspen, Miami, Dallas. They never shut up.

I get monthly stomach bugs and my Spanish is remarkably bad. I spend my weekends drinking and drugging away the sound of children's voices saying, *Meees* over and over again in my head. I like to think I'm living in my own short, black and white art film. I want this movie to titillate, but the truth is, it's boring and even slightly depressing.

Back home in California, I left behind my two sisters, my brother and sister-in-law to care for my sick mom. My mother is losing her memory. She didn't recognize me during my last visit in November. All five adults live together in one home. My siblings take turns caring for my mother. I told them I could no longer bear the heartache of seeing her change. I told them I needed space. So, I left.

I will feel the unspoken repercussions of my move to D.F. for several years. I might still feel it to this day.

Now, ten years later, I have a husband and a four-year-old daughter, and we live in Saigon, Vietnam, the same city where my mother once lived before she got sick. I came here for another terrible teaching job, quit before my contract ended, and swore to God I would never do another classroom teaching job again. It took ten years to learn this lesson. I am forever learning new lessons.

I came to Vietnam for a job, but I think I really came here in search of my mother. I see her everywhere—in the soft, shy smile on women's faces in the park, in the perfectly peeled slices of grapefruit at the fruit shop around the corner from my house, in a bowl of breakfast *Hủ Tiếu*. I can't explain why

I keep living abroad either, except that it feels like home, as an outsider looking in, just like my parents were as Vietnamese exiles in America. Perhaps it helps me understand my mother better, too.

I like myself a lot more than I did ten years ago on June 4th. I've forgiven myself for the many mistakes I made. I still believe in a good story. The only difference is, I'm spending my time writing them down, rather than chasing after them like I did before. I write about my family. My hope is that my sisters, my brother, and sister-in-law will one day read my completed story and maybe, then, they'll forgive the person I was ten years ago too.

"CHRISTIAN LOVE IS COMPLICATED WHERE IT SHOULD BE EASY"

Jasminum McMullen

June 4th, on the main floor of the 333 building, I found my way around the coffee bar and stepped into an empty hall. The yellowed track of light diffuses in the drop ceiling, casting a thin shadow in the narrow space outside the unoccupied conference rooms. I leaned against the wall and waited on hold. The receptionist answered my request to speak with the pastor by transferring my call to Reverend F. When he answered, I inquired about marriage services and access to the chapel. As a new Christian, the church building was essential to our wedding plans. And since I had the connection to the church, I took responsibility for the arrangements.

Reverend F: Well, we don't believe in that.

And he proceeded to convert me by asking if I had considered confessing Jesus Christ as my Lord and Savior. I reminded Reverend F that he preached a sermon on a first Sunday a year ago that moved me to join church and how much it meant to me. He paused. The silence between us, canyon-sized and deafening. I heard the gravel as his throat cleared. I inquired again about marriage services and access to the chapel. The

104

need to negotiate emerged hot, like something boiled in my belly. I went straight to deal mode and out quickly.

Me: We'd accept accommodations outside the chapel, perhaps in the SGDC?

(a separate building on campus).

Reverend F: We believe what the Bible says. A marriage is between a man and a woman.

But wasn't I also Christian? Did my relationship with God depend on how much I could hate sins, people, myself? And if I believed as a Christian that marriage between two women is possible and representative of Jesus's love, then on my authority as a woman of God, *we* do *believe in that*, I thought. I wanted our wedding, our union approved by God in a sacred place because our love is Holy.

Reverend F invited me to Bible study. And I couldn't help but wonder if he misinterpreted my request to use the chapel for our wedding as a desire to walk a path towards devotion to a common penis. Authority makes disasters of men who obsess over Dicks and Janes who don't want them. I thanked him, and our call ended. I felt severed, so, subtly labeled, not Christian.

She, who likes breasts, is more oppressed. Queerlations 13:1

Christian love is complicated in places where it should be easy.

I left the site of our conversation in darkness, pushed through the lobby doors, and into the light. The sun shone in a clear sky. I lit the cigarette I fished out of my pocket and smoked it down to the filter. I flicked the burning carcass into the breeze and prepared to return to work for the money God blessed me with to give to a church I loved enough to closet myself for because love required sacrifice.

Today, I sit on the pew and wonder why I ever thought God's love and approval was obtainable through a flawed man with a little office authority stuck on drawing a line in the sand between his definition of Christianity and my own. No, I am the church, and my relationship with God is precious and valid.

After the flood, Noah looked for signs the disaster was over. God said "This is the sign of the covenant I am making between me and you and every living creature with you, a covenant for all generations to come: I have set my rainbow in the clouds, and it will be the sign of the covenant between me and the earth."

"('TIL) I KISSED YOU"

Gaurra Shekhar

June 7th, on the eve of my fifteenth birthday, I stayed up answering questions on FormSpring, a now-defunct Q&A forum. Because FormSpring was anonymous, it was a big hit in our school—a kind of notes-slipped-into-your-virtual-locker-type thing. Except all questions and answers were published, presumably for awkward teens to feel momentary want and fame.

I'll confess I sent myself a few of the saucier public questions under the guise of anonymity. Okay, I sent myself a lot of them. Most of them. Really, this forum was an outlet to make myself seem desirable to the internet boys in school. So, when I received a legitimate question from an anonymous asker (a boy, I'd hoped), I lit up and put on a pot of coffee. *What's your favorite song of all time?* The question felt intimate, and soft. I considered my answer thoughtfully before typing out Modest Mouse's "Third Planet." Moments later, lyrics from the song sprung up on my Twitter feed: *the universe is shaped exactly like the earth / if you go straight long enough you'll end up where you were.* The question, as it turned out, was asked by a real boy, the one who kept trying (and failing) to make it onto the soccer team.

This was the most exciting thing to have happened to me all day, week, year, and, for all I knew, probably ever. I danced a caffeinated dance around my room and plopped onto the bed. How could I sleep now? I asked my iTunes library what my year was going to be like, and hit shuffle: the Everly Brothers'

"('Til) I Kissed You." That was enough for me, a song to portend the year of my first kiss.

The next decade of birthday eves would see me in tears, throwing up out of taxicab windows, eating leftover spaghetti on the bathroom floor, sending out 7 a.m. texts to exes, counting change for coffee at an airport, waiting for a flight that kept getting delayed. Fifteen didn't turn out to be the year of my first kiss, but I would inevitably return to the memory of listening to "('Til) I Kissed You" alone in my room, and wonder if I was happiest when my hair was bleached, and my dreams still lingered as a restless abstract potential of boys and bands.

Now that life is static and confined, my thoughts whirl like a hopeless spin at the Big Six. The pointer rubs against the night, stopping at no resolve. I think about how a body like mine has existed in space over the past decade, if I was happy where I've been, if I'm happy where I am now. I've been a college dropout and a graduate candidate. I've been an unpaid intern who hauled record shipments to USPS in the rain. I've been a person you poured your heart out to on the roof of your old apartment. I've been a person who left the country, a person who lost her passport on the way to City Hall the day she was supposed to get married, and sometimes, still: a person who expects a song to portend the year to come.

I'm about to turn twenty-five, quarantined in an apartment with my husband, at the epicenter of a pandemic that has put the world on pause. So much of this feels like fiction. I'm not sure what happens next, where we go, what we do, or write. It feels embarrassing to ask an iTunes algorithm to tell me what my future sounds like, so I don't. Instead, I hold on to the wild faith of the gesture, and tightly. At the very least, it's hope to build a dream on.

"ALL THE PEOPLE WHO SIMPLY WANT TO EXIST"

Natalie Byers

"**D**id you have something to add to the conversation, Natalie?" June 15th, I shook my head and jammed my lips together; I needed more time to process what had been said, consider how much the other students had actually read, dig down into my psyche, try not to punch anyone, and create a perfect, compound-complex sentence that succinctly described my opinion on the nature of queer theory.

So, instead of saying something, anything, I said nothing.

I let my chest tighten. I struggled to breathe, clenched my fist, bit my cheeks, and smoked two cigarettes with Bailey during the night class break.

"I think I'm a *," I told her. Pulled on a yellow, American Spirit, exhaled, stared out across the university green at the Brown Derby liquor store on the corner.

I didn't have a fucking clue what being a * meant.

In class though, there were fifteen straight, cis-gendered individuals who, apparently, did.

The week before, we discussed bell hooks' 1990 essay, "Postmodern Blackness." After no one else in the class volunteered to comment on the assigned reading, I posited that hooks' sentiment was wholly accurate; black folks fall into two categories: "nationalist or assimilationist, Black-identified or white-identified."

I spoke, probably too long, about code-switching. I pointed out several current examples of young Black men being portrayed as violent criminals in almost every type of media or entertainment, the exception being *Fresh Prince*, or maybe *White Men Can't Jump*. Essentially, I fully expected the entire class to applaud my amazing discovery that critical race theory was, in fact, American history.

Dr. Jane nodded her head enthusiastically at my revelations.

No one else said anything. I thought, perhaps, Dr. Jane was being polite, encouraging her student. So, the following week, when we discussed queer theory, I assumed I must certainly be a moron and I most definitely misread the assigned essay.

I'll just be quiet.

Shut my mouth.

Be amicable.

When other students posed that queer labels were too much, that things were just going too far, that men exist, that women exist, and that's that, I didn't think I had a valid opinion.

A student who prefaced their statement with "I'm a trans woman" continued to claim things were just out of control. "Calm down, already. Absolutely none of that matters."

Our professor nodded enthusiastically. "When is enough, enough? Is that what you're getting at?"

"Exactly," Drew responded. "Like, I just wanna live and let live, you know?"

That's when Dr. Jane asked me if I had anything to add. Clearly, my face was saying things that my mouth couldn't get out.

By the time Bailey and I finished our cigarettes, I knew what I wanted to say.

Maybe when people aren't being murdered for existing, we can debate what they want to be called when they were alive.

The second half of class went by, and I sat on my thesis statement. I drove home thinking about it. I drank myself to sleep thinking about it. When Dr. Jane died, I thought about it. At her funeral, I thought about it. Every time someone is assaulted for it, I think about it.

For ten years, I've thought about all the people who simply want to exist.

And I think about how I said nothing.

This essay has a 1000-word count limit, so I can't list all of the people who have died for existing—Black, brown, and or queer since then.

Now, I teach composition at a technical college in Missouri. I wish I could tell you what some of my students have said about people who aren't cis-gendered and white. That would be a privacy violation and I don't want to be tossed out of the only profession my six-figure-debt-education has prepared me for.

But, it's the Otherness of it all.

As if Mary Shelley never wrote *Frankenstein*.

Or Prince never played basketball.

And Freddy Mercury was straight.

"WHEN YOU FINISH THIS BOOK, YOU WILL DIE"

June Gervais

I had one superstition. Just one.

I am not generally superstitious, but at some point, this one appeared like moths nesting in the back of a cabinet. It was troubling and irrational; it *was* superstition, not intuition, and I *knew* that.

But it kept returning, an intrusive thought so morbid I kept it to myself:

When you finish writing your book, you will die.

The thing about intrusive thoughts is you can't always reason them away. When did this foreboding begin?—in my twenties, I think? At that point, I'd been puzzling out my novel for half a decade or so. I needed to finish; I'd made a promise to my teenage self, a girl with depression so severe she was hospitalized twice. This was my mantra: *I need to live, because I'm going to college, and I'm going to write a book that will make someone else feel less alone.*

But did I think this was the *sole* purpose of my life? Had I absorbed that cliché—*everyone dies when it's their time, when they've completed their mission on earth*—and decided this book was the *only* reason the universe kept me around?

I don't know. Sometimes I went months without thinking of the superstition, but I was always thinking of the book. Finally, in June of 2009—resolving to finish it, once and for all—I

112

entered an MFA program. And five days into the program, I discovered with joy that I was pregnant with my first child.

Clearly, I had a dual vocation now. I wasn't just here to put words on paper; I was here to welcome this child to planet Earth, with all its wonders, and be his tour guide for a while. I dreamed of him before he was born. He had huge, beautiful eyes, and I could tell that he was funny and kind.

He arrived, and it all turned out to be true, and more: he spoke early and clearly and took in the whole world with those big brown eyes. Our days were full of walks and blocks and books and *look at that!*

Look, Charlie, a motorcycle! What noise does it make?

Look, Charlie, the ocean! What does the water feel like?

Look, Mama, look! Yes, that's a starfruit. An old cicada shell. A mourning dove.

My superstition should've evaporated at this point, disappearing in a puff of its own weird logic. But sometimes—especially when I was nearing completion on a draft of my novel—it would start to materialize again, like smoke seeping under the door.

THIS BRINGS US TO JUNE, ten years ago.

If you *look, look*, in any given June, you're sure to see the signs of something bearing fruit. A wedding dress. A graduation cap. A strawberry field like an acre of rubies.

That June was one of those seasons for me, with more changes than I can recount here, hard and happy and both. Charlie was nearly two and a half, recently graduated from diapers—no longer a baby, but a boy who made us laugh by reciting lines from "The House that Jack Built," *This is the man all tattered and torn, who kissed the maiden all forlorn...*

I was about to complete the requirements for my master's degree. I'd been hired for a new job, slated to begin soon. And just a few weeks earlier, I'd accomplished the dream I'd labored over so long. I finished writing my book.

When you finish writing this book... I waved it away. Relic of old nonsense, anxiety in disguise. And there was so much else to do. Soon I'd drive to Vermont for my final MFA residency, heavenly Green Mountains in June, fresh air and fireflies. Years of work would culminate. I'd give a reading from my novel, and I'd give a lecture that I'd poured so much heart and soul into, it might as well have been a sermon. If all went well, later that day, I would put on a black robe and receive the diploma for my MFA.

I fretted and worried, but it *did* seem to go well. At the end of my lecture, my son yelled "YAY, MAMA!" and a hundred people laughed and shared my joy. We graduates graduated. At the party, my hungry boy ate a pile of buttered rolls, and I wore a red dress, red as the ripest June strawberry.

That day, June 23rd, was supposed to be the big day. It would mark the beginning of everything I'd been working toward: querying agents, seeing my book in print.

June 24th was supposed to be the day of catching my breath. After the ecstasy, the laundry. After the party, the goodbye. June 24th was just the day we'd pack up my little green Toyota Echo and go home.

I DON'T REMEMBER what my husband and I were talking about as we drove west. I do remember we were on a two-lane highway in upstate New York; that we'd been on the road for about an hour, and we were stressed. Details, maybe? Daycare, coordinating calendars, *Remind me when the new job starts?*

Charlie had a bout of hollering, weary of his car seat, and then he calmed down. The fields blurred by, soft with timothy, the air hazy. Every now and again: *Look, Charlie!* A river. A hawk. The fog.

A car.

Driving straight toward us, in the wrong lane, trying to pass the car in front of it.

The driver saw us too late. He tried to jerk back into his lane, but he fishtailed and lurched into ours again. He was heading straight across our path now, too fast for my husband to do anything but hit the brakes and try to veer right. We hurtled toward him.

In that flash of a moment before impact, everything in me went dead still. What happens in a moment like that cannot be called "thinking," exactly. But I did have an *oh* of understanding. *Oh. It was true. This is how I die.*

I closed my eyes. Our car slammed into his.

I opened my eyes, and I was alive.

Broken glass, limp airbags, crumpled metal. I didn't know I was hurt; nothing mattered but Charlie. The only thing I remember is jumping out, grabbing him from his car seat, running as fast as I could and yelling at my husband, *Get away from the car, get away.*

DURING THE COLLISION, I closed my eyes—but Charlie didn't.

Over the next few days, he told the story again and again, in slightly different versions. It was weirdly riveting. I wrote them down. If you transcribe a young child's speech, it sounds spookily like poetry.

The car hit us and we got boo-boos. We went outside on the grass and I can smell smoke and the smoke is beautiful. The cars came. Came to help us.

We went on the grass and drink water. Smoke coming out of a hole in Mama's car.

The car hit us and went to the hospital. They made you feel better. We went in the ambulance and drove.

I don't want the smoke. I don't want smoke to come out of Mama's car.

THE WAY CHARLIE'S WORDS circled around and around that year, trying to tell the whole story—*the smoke is beautiful... we went on the grass and drink water... I don't want the smoke...* Life feels like that to me, more like a spiraled labyrinth than the linear ticks of a timeline.

Every June 23rd, I remember the euphoria and completion and *Yay, Mama.* I remember the love in that lecture hall, which felt like a holy moment in my life, and led me to teaching. The joy of June 23rd is still electric for me.

And every June 24th, I think of the accident. The fishtailing car. Holding my son and running. I don't *like* thinking about it. Even as I type these words, fear darts through my body again.

But when I come around to June 24th, mostly what I feel is awe. That is the day we could have died, and we didn't.

Charlie is twelve now. He's told me that one of his first memories is drinking apple juice in an ambulance, but he says this matter-of-factly; it seems to carry no trauma.

My novel, it turned out, wasn't finished, and had a long road ahead. As I write this, though, a red hardcover rests on my desk. The cover shows a girl with streaks in her hair, red as a June strawberry—no, redder; July fireworks. An illustrated eye hovers above her. *Look. Look.*

The book is finished, and that no longer frightens me. When I made the last fiddling copy edit a year ago, on a summer day, no dark foreboding haunted me. Ten years ago, I had one superstition—but now I have none.

JULY

"I DON'T WANT HIM TO KNOT HER UP"

Jeni McFarland

July 5th, there's a man who shows up in all my quiet moments. While I drive to school, he sits in the back seat. He ducks down when cars pass, when I stop at traffic lights, when I enter or exit the car, when I look in the rearview, but I know he's there; I can hear him breathing, heavily. Sometimes I catch the balding top of his head, that dull, soft patch of skin, out of the corner of my eye, or just before he ducks entirely out of view.

At home, when I'm watching TV or having dinner with my fiancé—fish and vegetables, because I'm trying to shed some of the fat I've accreted over the years—the man squeezes himself between us on the couch. His leg touches mine, hip to calf. I can smell him; a damp, earthy mushroom smell that puts me back inside his bedroom when I was a child. The man doesn't say anything, and my fiancé doesn't mention the man, but I can tell his presence is wearing thin.

I talk to my mother on the phone, but the man shouts in the background.

"You are worthless," he yells. "Nothing you do matters." He's so loud, I have to ask my mother to repeat herself.

"You seem distracted," she says.

"It's the bald man," I say. "Don't you hear him?"

"I hear nothing," she says, but he shouts even louder, his spit hitting my cheek.

119

"Really," I say, "this is too much. You don't hear that?" He wrestles me for the phone.

"I don't hear anything," she says. "And neither do you."

Late at night the man feeds me—bacon cheeseburgers, a case of beer, a baker's dozen of Krispy Kremes, Gummy Bears, Oreos, pints of ice cream, potato chips, spilling bowls of popcorn, chocolate cake—shoves the food in then cups a hand over my mouth and nose until it's either swallow or suffocate. "That's right," he says. "That's a good girl."

I try to sleep, and he stands at the foot of my bed, whispering, "You are worthless, you are nothing," until my face is wet and hot.

The man wakes my fiancé, who tells the man, "Shut up. Don't make me come over there."

The man shuts up for a while. My fiancé holds me, and finally I sleep. But in the morning, the man is still there, breathing, watching me undress. He undresses too, a ritual he started when I was a child, but I keep an eye on him. I pull on gym clothes, tennis shoes, and the man throws himself down, naked, flabby, and holds onto my ankles.

"You can't have this," he says. "None of it. You deserve none of it."

And he's right. I'm planning a wedding I can't afford, studying for a bachelor's degree I'll never get. I'm marrying into a family of PhDs. My maid-of-honor is away, studying for her PhD. She's also getting married, a month before me. I am not her maid-of-honor. And it's my fault, I know. Because of the company that keeps me, I'm guarded and weird; I don't tell her about myself, I don't tell anyone anything, I worry she'll find out about the man who's been following me since I was a child, that somehow, he'll infect her with some of the same sickness, that fear that worms inside me until it grows hard and dark as a tree-knot.

I don't want him to knot her up, because then what if he follows her around too, saying, "I still own you"?

"WHY I'D NEVER DATED"

Vonetta Young

No man had ever loved me, not even my father. So, ten years ago on July 11th, my fingers hovered above my keyboard, trying to decide what to put on my OkCupid profile. I was twenty-two years old and desperate to finally start dating. I needed to know I was loveable.

I'd had crushes, but all of my pining went unexpressed and unrequited. When my mom said I could start dating when I turned fifteen, I circled my birthday on my calendar, praying someone would ask me out that very day, but to no avail. I went through high school and college without going on a date.

What was wrong with me?

On OkCupid, I said I was big into reading, dancing, and Jesus. My heart thumped in my ears when I got a match and arranged a date. But he stood me up, further confirmation that something was wrong with me.

Then a friend set me up with a guy who'd messaged her on Yelp. He liked to dance, so maybe he was my type. She helped me craft a message to him.

A week later, we met at the chicest nightclub in D.C. He bought me a drink but had water himself, health conscious and frugal. He was a socialist, which was fascinating. When I said I was a capitalist, he grimaced, jokingly. We danced until morning, when the lights revealed us both as sweaty, but attractive. He walked me home, and we kissed in front of my building.

It wasn't love, but a man I was attracted to was attracted to me: a dream come true.

HE TOOK ME OUT almost every weekend that summer. During the week, we emailed; he lived with his mother and didn't like to talk on the phone because she might hear. I admired that he was saving money to buy a house. My rent was too damn high, anyway, I joked.

"Why don't you just move somewhere cheaper," he snipped. This made sense, but his tone grated me.

At the end of summer, he emailed explaining why I'd never dated: I was too concerned with dressing nicely, cared too much about what he thought of me, was too politically conservative, believed in Jesus and capitalism, had credit card debt, drank too much, gave into peer pressure, didn't exercise, and wanted to spend money traveling.

I blinked at the screen. If these things were the problem, the only thing I'd done wrong was to be myself. He apologized for judging me, but I told him to not talk to me anymore. It was the end of my first relationship. It lasted only two months.

I am lovable and someone is going to love me for me, I told myself. But I spent fall and winter enraged, wondering if being me would always be insufficient.

One spring Friday, at a bar, I saw a guy, Rustin, who'd gone to my university. We danced and talked until our friends left us. We drank water because we'd both given up alcohol for Lent. We exchanged drunk study abroad stories. I confessed my shopping habit; Rustin laughed, saying he'd happily overuse my Banana Republic employee discount.

When Rustin called me on Sunday, I hesitated. Then I recalled how he'd shared his flaws and didn't shame me for mine. It was like he'd wanted me to be me. I answered the phone. Now, we've been married for six years, traveled the world, paid off our debt, drank too much, exercised, shopped, and debated intelligently about politics and religion. Rustin has gone out of his way to prove I am worthy of love, even on those days when I can't quite believe him.

"MISS GAYLE CUT HER HAIR"

Wandeka Gayle

"Wandeka, is that you?"

I turned to find my former college roommate, staring, slack-jawed, at my hair. It was July 12th.

I ran a hand over my shorn curls with a sigh. She'd never seen me with shoulder-length hair, but I knew how strange I must look to her with my hair so closely shaven that I looked like a plucked chicken.

I cringed then just as I did when I walked into the classroom with my new haircut a few months before.

"Miss Gayle cut her hair... Look, she cut her hair... Watch deh!"

Murmurs rippled alongside me as I walked to the front of the class.

Then, one brave soul addressed me directly, "Miss Gayle, is you cut it yourself?"

I smiled at the surge of laughter. I had thought it innocent enough, for I could not then see the patches where my scalp peeked through. It looked like I had cut it with a pair of dull craft scissors using a one-way mirror under a weak light.

That's because I had.

I had never been attached to my hair, but this seemed a volatile act. I could blame it on a weeklong flu-induced stupor that created the matted monstrosity I could not bring myself to tackle with a comb.

Perhaps it was somehow the physical representation of a very disappointing period in my life. I had not taken up a paint brush in months, nor written a word of fiction, nor played a single new note on piano. Plus, teaching, intended to last just one semester, had stretched into a full year and a half and I had begun to despise research essays, run-on sentences, or trying to convince them "writing" didn't have two t's.

Most of all, I had not applied to graduate school as planned. I would picture myself walking across a stage once again in full regalia, but I would not apply, part from fear, part from complacency. I also couldn't imagine living anywhere but Jamaica.

That ordinary day in July, ten years ago, walking along the piazza, and facing this specter from my past, I knew I appeared externally as far removed from the sensible, consistent person I had been in college.

"Of course, it's me!" I said. "Just needed a change is all."

She could have said something reassuring but that had never been her style. She had always been blunt even with misguided good intentions. I remembered that this was the same woman who a day after swatting terms for her medical terminology test unceremoniously diagnosed me with halitosis because of something as benign as morning breath.

So, I decided I would not allow myself to feel diminished by her look of horror.

"What have you been up to?" she asked, seeming to recover slightly.

"I'm teaching up at the university and I still write features for a magazine and for *The Gleaner*," I said.

It was in articulating these things to her that I realized things had not been as dismal as I had casted them in my mind.

I was twenty-five and I was doing okay.

If I could reach back to that self of a decade ago, I'd squeeze her into an embrace, tell her everything happens within its own time, that two years later we do leap for the master's degree, and that in ten years would be chronicling the immigrant experience in a dissertation.

"We do cut our hair again. Many times," I'd say. "And we look fabulous."

"I AM A HUMAN BOWLING BALL"

Jenn Jones Sutliff

That July 22nd, I looked down at the three swollen incisions on my abdomen and thought, *I am a human bowling ball.* The incisions lay delicately on each side of my stomach with one tiny hole living in my belly button. They itched and burned, but it was better than the utter heaviness and pain I had been living with for the past year. I tried to sit up in the hospital bed, ignoring the slight sting of pain as I struggled. The nurse adjusting my IV broke into a huge grin as she helped me sit up. She asked how I was feeling.

I felt hollowed out, scraped clean. I had been both of those things more or less the past year, but hopefully this time, that feeling would be gone for good. I imagined myself as one of those watermelon centerpieces at parties, filled with cubes of fruit so people could pick at me with their toothpicks while they laughed and talked and didn't pay any mind to the emptied-out woman in front of them. *Don't mind me*, I would say as they stabbed at me with their little wooden sticks and carried on with their conversation.

This is normal!

That thought had been in my greatest hits rotation for the past year, along with:

Oh, we're going to freeze my cervix and scrape some cells off of it?
This is normal!

Oh, we're going to numb me, attach an electrode to my thigh, and cut out pieces of my cervix without any general anesthesia while I am awake?

This is normal!

Oh, okay, so we're going to inflate me like a balloon and root around inside my uterus?

This is normal!

People like a real can-do attitude these days.

Of course, I don't tell the nurse this. I opted for an awkward, painkiller-addled thumbs up. Nobody wants to hear you complain about being a centerpiece or your reproductive issues at eight in the morning. In this economy? Forget it.

The door swung open and in strode my doctor, clipboard in hand and smiling. We had become a team, the two of us, over the last twelve months against team Don't You Want A Baby? Something funny happens when you get diagnosed with reproductive issues. Everyone around you graduates from the Google School of Modern Medicine with a minor in I Know It's Just My Opinion But. The key to ending endometriosis and potential ovarian cancer according to these esteemed scholars? Pregnancy. Just have a baby, my then-mother-in-law said, talking over my head to my then-husband as I stood in front of her, won't that get rid of her "issues"?

I had become invisible, as my ability to incubate a human and shoot it out of me like a T-shirt out of one of those cannons at basketball games was clearly in peril. Never mind the raised cancer antigen levels in my blood work or the fact I couldn't take a step without lightning rods of pain shooting up my back and legs. Won't someone think of the uteruses?

Doc checked a few things on my chart as she sat down in a chair next to the bed. She grinned. "We got it all," she said, patting my arm, as she went over the procedure.

I'd had tissue growing outside of my uterus. It wrapped around my uterus, bladder, rectum, both ovaries and both fallopian tubes. It had spread out like vines, invading my body, threatening to fuse my organs together. It had formed a tight little ball that compressed against my sciatic nerve that made every step I took agony. I closed my eyes as she continued to tell me about my defective, heart-shaped uterus and my dead ovary and fallopian tube that now lay in a lab somewhere. I let it all wash over me, eyes closed. When she finished, she told me it was the worst case of endometriosis she had seen yet. I opened my eyes, still feeling toasty from my painkiller cocktail.

"Hey, doc," I asked, "you can see me, right?"

"Yes, she said, chuckling, "yes, I can see you."

I laid back in bed and shut my eyes in relief.

"THE LONG BOAT RIDE HOME"

Damien Miles-Paulson

That July 26th, I was twenty-eight and living in an old lightkeeper's house on San Juan Island, the lighthouse long ago automated. My daughter, Isabella, was almost eight, and that summer I couldn't afford to send her to daycare, so she came to work with me. I was working for Washington State Parks then, and much of my job consisted of taking a boat to different islands: Jones Island, Blind Island, Turn Island, Stuart Island—and there I'd clean bathrooms, mow lawns or do small projects. While I worked, Isabella looked after herself, and though I knew she'd be fine, each day I told her to stay on the beach, to stay away from the water.

On Jones Island, there were apple orchards, leftovers from a failed homestead, and in late summer when the apples were ready I'd climb up into the trees and shake the apples out, and as Isabella picked them up, deer rushed out of the forest. I'd jump down and try to chase the deer away, but they were unafraid of me.

All the toilets on these islands were composting toilets that I had to maintain by hand. When these toilets were emptied into a large finishing bin it was called downloading. Once a summer, I had to stir and rotate the previous summer's shit. By year three, the shit had become night soil, compost, and I'd throw it into the salal bushes.

128

At the end of each day, on the long boat ride home, tired from the sun, lulled by the motion of the boat planing over the water, Isabella would fall asleep on a pile of lifejackets I had laid out, and even when we skipped over a large wake from a passing ferry, sending her into the air, she never woke up. Those moments made me feel like a good parent.

When Isabella would leave the island to stay with her mother, I barely spoke.

I drove to the library and wrote emails to distant friends saying things like:

A man disappeared from Jones Island. His boat was left anchored in North Cove, his dinghy tied to the dock, no sign of him, his wallet and passport gone. He was sixty and maybe while crossing the Spieden Triangle he saw three harbor porpoises and an eagle and he killed the motor and just listened. He hadn't listened for years, so much had passed unnoticed, as if he had been deaf. He said, "I'm going to disappear," and after anchoring his boat and tying his dingy to the dock he swam away. Well, that is the romantic take. The way I'd like his story to end, with a beginning, with a sprint through the final years of his life. Perhaps that is the kind of thing I have in store for me.

And:

I haven't felt the need. My inspiration and imagination have receded like my hair. No longer can I make up. A narrative comb-over.

The ferry from San Juan to Orcas Island on a market weekend. The rain. Friends, and everywhere the sound of internal combustion. Two young girls laugh in a library. They laugh so loud that they cannot be quieted. I'm reminded of being underwater.

And thirty approaches, as does twenty-nine or thirty-five. What does it matter?

I paint a small wooden bathroom on an island visited by a handful of well-to-do people each year. I forget. The calls come less and less. I disappear from even my own memory. I don't recognize myself in the plots, characters, narratives and scenes of the books I read. Isabella walks up to me and cares nothing for what I have written to you. She asks for permission to walk down to the beach,

I consent, and she swipes my sunglasses from my face. I squint like a mole emerging from his hole. "Oh, funny face, Daddy. The whales . . . I think they're passing."

I want to sit at my small kitchen table with you and smoke cigarettes (a few but not enough to stink up the whole house) and drink good green tea or coffee or wine or beer or water and converse seriously enough to remind us that we are not completely full of shit, to remind us that we do more than repeat ourselves. We can pour the warm beers on the raccoons digging through the garbage cans just below the kitchen window and laugh. Even if we are serious we are still cruel and happy and beautiful for it.

It was a quiet time. I read and smoked cigarettes when I could afford a pack; and when I couldn't afford smokes, I would search my car ashtray for butts. Every cigarette was burned down to the filter.

AUGUST

"THAT NAME, HOBART, STUCK WITH ME"

Aaron Burch

I'm thirty-two years old, on summer break. This time next year, I'll have my MFA and will be driving up the California coast on my honeymoon, but right now I'm in Sacramento, having just driven up the California coast on a reading tour. Lindsay flew home a couple of days ago, after San Diego and Los Angeles and the first of two back-to-back reading dates in San Francisco, and we've been reading with various friends in every city, but now it's just me and Amelia. Tonight—August 5—will be a disaster. A reading at a café that got triple-booked alongside trivia night and some kind of networking event. I'll think absolutely no one is there for us, but over the years I'll hear from a couple of people who were actually there, and I'll love them for it, but tonight, as it is all happening, or *not*-happening, it will seem ridiculous and frustrating and pointless to even try and read and so, something of a brat, I won't. Amelia, however, will get up on a chair or maybe a table or maybe she stays on the ground but I'll remember her as elevated, in the air and in command, and she'll yell her story at everyone, a reading that will feel the exact right amount of ridiculous and frustrated and pointless. After, we'll go out for drinks with the handful of people who organized the event, but by then, we're over it. We hate Sacramento and our sleeping situation for the night seems sketchy at best and so sometime after midnight we make a spur of the moment decision to get out of Dodge—we pay our tab and we get in the car we rented for the tour and drive two hours to Reno, where we sleep at a friend of a friend's who has a Murphy bed, the only one I've ever seen in real life. Tomorrow I'll go rafting down the Truckee River with my friend, Gabe, and that night we'll go out gambling and Gabe will teach us how to play craps and after that; Amelia and I will hit the road again, the final leg of our drive, all the way back down to Tucson, where we'll stay with her parents and then do an event with Spork that, like all things Spork, is pretty impossible to try and describe.

THERE'S A STORY I'VE WRITTEN about a handful of times, and have told countless more. I grew up in youth group and on one weekend retreat, shortly after we arrived at the cabin and were being given a tour, about to be shown the kitchen and its giant dishwashers, where helping with dishes would be one of our weekend chores, one of my buddies looked at a couple of us and said, "I bet they have a Hobart." That always stuck with me. It's been twenty-five years, at least, and I still remember that moment like it's a scene from a movie I've rewatched countless times over the years. Which, in a sense, it kind of is. That name, Hobart, stuck with me; I always thought it might be a good band name. It's a single word, it sounds mysterious but also familiar, while not being sure why. When I started a lit journal shortly after undergrad, I gave it that name, thinking starting a lit journal was probably the closest I'd ever be to being in a van. This California (and Tucson) tour is the third I've done with Amelia and Lindsay in a little over a year, after having so much fun on our first and so planning another, and then another, and it feels a little like that dream of being in a band. Touring the country in vans and rented cars, having amazing events, suffering through horrible ones, going to bars and cafes and casinos, the long hours of drives in between, crashing on the floor and couches and Murphy beds of friends and friends of friends and parents... It's all a little ridiculous and sometimes frustrating or seemingly pointless but other times some of the most fun ever and it's exhausting and amazing and chaotic. It's perfect.

"LOOKING THE PART"

Michael Nye

Ten years ago, August 5th was a Thursday, the first week of the month, a workday between the summer and autumn semesters at the University of Missouri. There were no students on campus and most of my staff that worked the summer were also away; my boss and his wife were almost certainly on a vacation. The Department of English was temporarily housed there, though the offices of professors, lecturers, and graduate students were certainly empty. I don't remember what other departments were in the building then, but those offices too were likely unoccupied then.

This building was McReynolds Hall, where I worked for more than five years at a literary magazine called the *Missouri Review*. McReynolds was a long, rectangular brick building with square metal windows. Concrete steps lead to a concrete platform to enter the building; below these platforms is a gravel ravine that slopes toward the sub-level basement windows. Originally built as a dormitory and cafeteria in 1956, McReynolds has long been used as a temporary space for departments to squat for a few months when their regular building on campus is being renovated. Since it was used primarily for overflow, maintenance on the building was a low priority; flooding and persistent mold were common.

From my office window, my view was of a parking lot and the university power plant. Located on the top floor and southwest corner of a four story, flat-roofed building, my office would heat up early in the morning, the air conditioner kicking on and whirling all day long, never succeeding in cooling the room. I took my paperwork to another room—a small library down the hall or a cavernous meeting room on the third floor—and tried to concentrate.

It was during this three-week period when I would give up wearing a suit and tie. I wore such a professional outfit to an office where my boss wore faded polo shirts and tattered jeans almost every day. I liked wearing a suit. I liked how it distinguished me from everyone else. This was during a period where suits were back in vogue, thanks to shows like *Mad Men*. Today, my suits and ties and dress shirts hang in my closet, untouched for five months and counting, as I work from home in a T-shirt and basketball shorts during a global pandemic.

A few months early that summer, I got engaged. We never married; I ended the relationship a few months later. My fiancée and I had renewed our lease on an apartment we both hated. The parking lot of our building was a narrow strip between sidewalk and brick building, with just a few parking spots and a dumpster that sat adjacent to the street, hot steam rising off the macadam. I had expected my engagement to be triumphant and buoying, but I quickly found it left me feeling remarkably blank.

What I remember of this time, then, is empty buildings. I, too, was an empty vessel, looking the part, or at least trying to, dimly aware that something was wrong.

Now I think of that period, ten years ago, as the end of my adolescence. This seems silly on a timeline: then I was thirty-one years old. However, I'm not sure I really made choices so much as I followed an outdated plan. It was as if I had researched, planned, and purchased a long trip that other people told me I must take, and I was standing at the boarding station, watching the train roll in, and realizing that I had never really wanted to take this particular journey in the first place.

There are no details to this particular date that I can point to definitively. All that remains is a feeling: dread, discomfort, and the growing fear that my life was about to change forever in a way that I did not want.

"I YEARN FOR MORE FROM
THIS INTERVIEW"

Cherryl Jensen

On August 12th, Mom sits in a puffy gray hospital chair
next to her bed in the Orchard Manor nursing home in
Lancaster, Wisconsin. She leans back, as if she doesn't have the
strength to hold herself up. Her oversized blouse sags, revealing
the scar from her open-heart surgery several years earlier. Her
skin is crackly white, like a china cup that has been broken and
glued back together. She isn't wearing her false teeth, and her
mouth hangs open, looking like an endless black hole.

I sit in a chair next to Mom as my brother-in-law videotapes
us. My voice is soft, persistent. It is the professional voice I
used so often when I interviewed people for the many stories
I wrote. Stories about college professors and their research at
universities in Iowa, Michigan, Washington, New Hampshire.
Feature articles about interesting people for the daily newspaper
in Yakima, Washington, and Keene, New Hampshire.

This story, however, my mother's story, is personal. I care how
she answers my questions—or doesn't. She hesitated when I
broached the idea of interviewing her. "What kinds of questions?" she asked. "Just questions about your life," I said.

I knew what she was afraid of. Would I ask why she beat
me with a branch from the maple tree in the front yard of our
house in Andrew, Iowa? Why she pricked Pam's arms with

pins as we watched TV on a Sunday night. Why she jumped out of the car after fighting with Dad.

I do not ask my mother these questions. Now is not the time. There would never be a time. I cannot bring these events into her dying days. And I fear she will deny them, or say she doesn't remember, making me doubt my own memories once again.

Instead, I ask about her childhood, the loss of her father when she was only ten, how she met Dad, the happiest days of her life, the saddest. I am not surprised by her answers. I knew she grew up poor and took lard sandwiches to school for lunch. And that Dad and she, in the first years of their marriage, lived on a farm and had four children under the age of five in a house with no running water. "We made do with what we had," she says more than once.

She says, after she graduated high school, she wanted to train to be a nurse, but they didn't have enough money. Now I'm surprised. I never thought of my mother desiring anything more than what she had—marriage and children. It never occurred to me that perhaps she wanted more, that she might even consider a profession.

But I yearn for more from this interview. I wonder if she wanted kids, if she is proud of us. She says that's what people did in those days, have kids. And she is proud of us because we are all hard workers. I don't ask if she loves us, if she loves me. I am afraid of the answers.

When the interview is over, I close my notebook, give D.A. the sign that he can stop the videotape. I will fly home to Michigan the next day.

"Are you coming back?" Mom asks.

"No. No, I don't think so."

We both know the next time I come home will be for her funeral.

Her brown eyes, deep in their sunken sockets, stare at me, as if she is trying to remember my face. I want to cry. I want to hug her. But I do nothing, just sit silently, feeling my face sag into letting go.

I do not hold my mother's searching gaze. I turn away and leave. I had hoped she would say she loved me. I couldn't bring myself to say I loved her.

IT HAS BEEN TEN YEARS since I interviewed my mother. She died a few months later. Only this year did I have the courage to look at this videotape. What was I afraid of? That I would be too sad? Or not sad enough?

"TEN YEARS LATER, AND I STILL CAN'T GET ENOUGH"

Abigail Thomas

August 12

Ten years ago I was obsessed. It was a little odd, and I can't explain it, but all I wanted to do, and all I did, was make paintings of fried eggs, sunny side up. I made individual egg portraits, group egg portraits, paintings of eggs snuggling together, families of eggs placed side by side, eggs dressed as ghosts for Halloween. I painted on glass with oil-based house paint that came in quarts. Despite all the other colors, it was yellow that called to me. Dipping a stick into the thick oily paint, then holding it steady above the glass, I could produce a perfect circle, drop by drop. It was magic. When the yolk was firm, I added the white. I could never have done it on purpose—some things only come about by accident, but in one particular painting, two little eggs wound up with strings attached. Somehow I had produced two small fried eggs on pogo sticks. I was so proud. I felt a little like their mother. I'm still in love with them, ten years later. God, I had a good time. I love obsession.

These days I do a lot of nothing. I'm good at doing nothing, but when I'm done doing nothing, I don't know what to do. We're in the middle of a pandemic. There's nowhere to go. I haven't driven my car in months. I should pay my taxes, call the septic guy, write some letters, pay my bills, but I am paralyzed. Let's see. Today. It's five-fifteen in the morning. What do I do? I pull a few hairs out of my head and hold them up to the light to make sure I don't have head lice. Sometimes the follicles look like nits, so I use a magnifying glass for closer examination. One of my younger grandsons has head lice, and my head is itching. Seven hairs, no lice. It's almost disappointing so I pull out another bunch of hair. Still no lice. My interest wanes. Then I pick up a catalog and look at mattress pads. For years I've longed for the fleece ones that they say are washable but I don't believe it, and I don't need a new mattress pad. Then I look at feather beds which I also don't need, although they look inviting. I drop the catalog back on the floor.

I keep reminding myself that a funk can be lifted by making something, anything, that's outside myself, but these days all I make are deviled eggs. Three eggs are boiling on the stove, I am chopping red onion into little chunks, I take the eggs out of the pot, thrust them into cold water, gently, carefully peel them, slice them in half and remove the yolks into a bowl of mayo and chopped onion, mix it all together and spoon it back into the egg whites. I slide the delicious little things into my mouth one after another, after another, day after day. Ten years later, and I still can't get enough.

"THAT DRIVE FROM KANSAS"

Brandon Daily

August 14

It's late afternoon when we leave Wichita. A couple of hours earlier, while I was packing, Mike, my team manager, called and told me I'd be driving one of the three minivans home. "You're the oldest player," he said.

I hung up and realized what that meant: I was no longer one of the young guys, and I never would be again.

We came to Wichita to play in the NBC World Series, a baseball tournament for semi-professional teams made up of college players. During the drive from California to Kansas, I stayed silent while the other guys talked about the colleges they'd be returning to in the fall. But I had already graduated. For me, the trip was different. For me, it was a last chance.

Three months prior to the trip, I was cut from a professional team in Michigan. Playing pro-ball had always been my dream, and for a few weeks, I knew what it felt like to hold that dream in my hands and call it real. When it didn't last, I came home to California lost, ready to give it up. But then Mike called, asking me to play for his semi-professional team. I said I was done with the game, that I was too frustrated. He told me to stick it out a little longer. "If we make it to Wichita," he said, "see if any scouts talk to you."

And so I agreed.

But Wichita didn't work out: we lost in four games and no scout talked to me.

WITHIN AN HOUR OF LEAVING, nearly everyone in my van is asleep. The empty nothingness of the Midwest passes by outside. Flat and calm, the opposite of my mind, which is constant with thoughts and worry. And fear. When I turn on the radio, John Mellencamp sings about growing up and moving on, and though I don't believe in signs from above, I wonder if this might be one.

And so I drive. Afternoon fades away and dusk creeps along, and then night, ushered in like a bruise on the western horizon that I drive toward.

While the night darkens and the radio goes to static, I feel the tears running down my cheeks.

But that's not the end of the story.

In New Mexico, I watch the most brilliant sunrise I've ever seen. Night is erased, and I find myself thinking of my girlfriend, Amanda, who is flying home that night from a study abroad trip in England.

I'll meet her at LAX and surprise her with roses. I'll wrap my arms around her, and I'll realize in that moment that baseball was never my only dream.

Over the next ten years, life will continue. I'll marry Amanda, and we'll have two children: a son and a daughter. In that time, I'll find a love of literature, and I'll lose myself within characters and plots and find that these stories bring me a sense of contentment, a way to understand my world. And I'll follow this passion like I once followed baseball, and I'll become a teacher of literature and publish stories and books. That's not to say all will be good in those ten years: Amanda will have four miscarriages, my mom will be diagnosed with breast cancer, and my brother will have a stroke, and this will change him and my family forever.

Often in those ten years, I'll find myself trying to reconcile the good and the bad, and I'll realize how that drive from Kansas gave me a microcosmic understanding of the world:

you drive through the dark knowing that the light will be there eventually, and it will wrap you in its arms and allow you to understand that the darkness is not all there is. There is also hope. There is always hope.

SEPTEMBER

"A PIVOT IN MY IDENTITY"

Kim Magowan

Ten years ago I emerged from the tunnel of small children at home to stare, blinking, at the future. I was forty-three years old, and I'd only recently stopped counting my youngest daughter's age in months.

We'd recently started Camille at pre-school three months after her second birthday because she wanted to be with older sister Nora, soon to begin kindergarten. Every time I picked the girls up, I'd find them holding hands. Miss Evelyn, their teacher, told me that Camille would play happily for an hour, but then approach some teacher or older kid, and say, "Take me to my Nora."

In Jenny Offill's novel *Dept. of Speculation*, the narrator describes the way having small children bends time, how it "cuts my day into little scraps." I had badly wanted children. I began dating my husband when I was thirty-six. Bryan was in his second year at UC Berkeley, on a demanding tenure clock. If he'd been with someone his age, instead of five years older, no question Bryan would have waited until tenure to have children. Nora was born a month before I turned thirty-eight, and by then I had been pregnant for half the time Bryan and I had been together.

During the first two and a half years of Nora's life, Bryan worked seven days a week—surgeon hours. I had the best babysitter on the planet, but Adam principally covered me when I was teaching or grading for the classes I taught at

Mills College as an adjunct instructor. Otherwise, it was me spending long hours in sandboxes. My mother called Camille my "barnacle" because she was always attached to me, nursing or in the Ergo carrier I wore so often that I felt, when I was without Camille, as if I had forgotten my clothes.

Between both girls in school and my teaching done until fall, time felt plentiful—a feeling I hadn't experienced since college. Nothing huge (dissertation-shaped) or small (those endless "scraps" Offill refers to) claimed me. And I felt an imperative pressure to get back to creative writing, something I had not devoted energy to for almost two decades.

At forty-three, I took stock. I loved my job, but it was a job, not a career (unlike my husband's). I loved my family and was watching them wheel away from me, in the perfectly developmental way they should. Statistically, my life was half over. My ambition flared again, a blue, insistent flame. I wanted to write. Moreover, I wanted people to read my fiction.

I'd submitted stories in my early twenties but had gotten demoralized—I was too dumb to realize then that a personal note rejection from the Paris Review was something to be proud of. It's always been easy to preempt rejection by not extending myself. Attempting to move past preemptive rejection, I wrote a new story that summer. When I showed it to my sister, she said, "What happens next?" Baffled, I said, "The story's over," but then I realized it was over from that particular character's perspective. If I switched POVs, it could continue. New possibilities opened, contingent on what choices that new character made. If he chickened out, this would happen. But if he took a chance... The story got very "choose-your-own adventure" as I pursued without understanding what I was chasing, the emerging paths I continued to create. It was a story about dissatisfying endings but also about second chances, both of which I was wrestling with myself, wondering what happens next or thinking I'm not good enough.

September 1st, I dropped my daughters at their schools, the oldest now on her own, with no little sister to nurture and cling to (of course I realized Nora clung back to Camille, just as I did, both arms around my Barnacle). September 1, I sent that oddball story that kept forking in unpredictable directions to *The Gettysburg Review.* They accepted it six months later—my first "ACCEPT!" on my submission spreadsheet, now nearly fifty pages long, mostly rejections.

September 1, for me marks a pivot in my identity, already hybrid and messy—teacher-wife-mom. I dropped off the girls, went home, prepared my next day's lecture, and then wrote for a couple of hours. That day, I became a writer.

"SOMETIMES I AM STILL UNKIND TO WHO I USED TO BE"

Diannely Antigua

September 4th, I was two days away from turning twenty-one. I was a virgin. I'd never been drunk. And I was about to venture on the most life-changing experience any young adult could fathom at the time: I was going to study abroad.

It sounds like the start of a YA novel—the girl is away from home for the first time, most likely falls in love, even more likely gets her heart broken, but ultimately finds herself. As the daughter of a librarian, I have seen these books countless times. I have read these books. And now I was about to live these books.

To truly understand who I was ten years ago is to understand who I was the ten years before that. I was raised in a strict religious system, one that had infiltrated every aspect of my life. For the last ten years, I had been the picture of a devout Christian girl: I went to church three times a week, I prayed and read my Bible every day, I didn't drink, I didn't curse, I didn't wear pants, I didn't listen to secular music, I didn't have sex. I had never lived outside of the repressive bubble created to keep me safe. I had been sheltered from the cruel world in the cruelest way. And it was all going to change. I was ready.

Or so I thought. The weeks leading up to my trip to Spain, I packed and repacked my bags, all with new unholy clothes, clothes to become someone I always wanted to be. I packed a

150

bottle of coconut lime body spray next to my new green bikini. I packed an ivory dress in case I fell in love and eloped.

Naïve would have been a generous word to describe myself. Stupid? Too harsh. I was somewhere in between. I was naïve because I had never been given the tools in which to maneuver as a woman in the modern world. I was stupid because I somehow thought I'd make it unscathed. Ill-equipped as I was, I would survive the trip, at some points maybe even flourish. It would be a painful amount of growth to happen to an ex-cult kid, to live one-life's worth of "worldly" adolescence in one semester. I would evolve into a woman, less pure, more angst-y, with still so much life yet to live. I had attempted to play catch-up with my past and would have to learn how to live in the present.

Sometimes I am still unkind to who I used to be. I hate the girl who doesn't know the name of that pop song from 2005, or the girl who still thinks of marriage when a first date goes well, or the girl who still feels like a mermaid discovering her legs every time she puts on a pair of jeans.

Or the girl who is still in therapy after eight years of trying to repair the damage left behind.

I remember this all as a woman on the brink of turning thirty-one, as a woman who will be moving into her first apartment on her own, as a woman with invisible disabilities, as a woman of color living in a world institutionally structured to oppress people like me.

And there is no YA novel to prepare me for this.

"I DIDN'T MEAN TO"

Veronica Daehn Harvey

Ten years ago on September 11th, I was not honoring those killed in the attacks on the World Trade Center. If I'm being honest, I probably wasn't even thinking about them, about those people who jumped out of the burning buildings, about the daycare center on the first floor, about the undergraduate college class I was driving to when I heard the news on the radio.

No. On that particular September 11th, I was thinking about my kids and about myself. Because my own world was falling down.

On that particular September 11th, my marriage was over, yet we were still figuring out how to untie all the threads that kept us living in the same house, angry, scared, hurt. Together, we had a four-month-old baby girl and a four-year-old boy. Our marriage was over because I'd cheated. I was an adulterer. I'd had an affair.

I didn't mean to. I wasn't looking for that. I just loved the attention. The last time I lived with my dad, I was twelve. My mom had left him, and I chose to go with her because of location, not because I loved my dad less. But having a dad twice a year does not give an adolescent girl what she needs when it comes to respecting her body or making smart choices.

My husband and I met during our freshman year in college. He was smart, charming, and confident. He was also controlling and emotionally abusive. He forced me to stop talking to my high school ex-boyfriend, even though we were only friends. He got angry when I wore, in his words, "tight white T-shirts." He didn't like my job as a lifeguard because I had to wear a swimsuit. He was the definition of insecure.

Ten years in, I broke. I was an editor at a major metro daily. My reporter flirted with me; he was relentless with his attention. Eventually, I gave in.

I will forever be ashamed. Even now, I fight urges to email his wife and tell her the truth. He never did, as far as I know.

So that day ten years ago, I was scared my husband might hurt me. I slept on my son's floor at night because I hoped I'd be safe there. One Saturday, my son and I came home from the pumpkin patch to a fire in the backyard. My husband was burning my things.

"What are you doing?" I asked.

"Hurting you like you hurt me," he said.

I began sleeping in the basement, baby monitor next to my head.

I drank too much. I cried too much.

Not for the victims of the terrorist attacks. No. For me and my babies and even my husband. I had ruined so much.

He moved out on January 1st. The house was so empty, and a piece of me was forever shattered.

For the first time in nearly a decade, though, I could breathe.

TEN YEARS LATER, we have both remarried. My second husband is patient, loyal, forgiving, and kind. My babies are fourteen and ten, and they have a half-sister, who just turned five. My ex-husband and I are civil most of the time, but he has not forgiven me. I have not forgiven him.

The world keeps spinning, on and on, regardless.

I often think back to that time of my life, to those choices I made. I often think, *Oh my God, who was that?* and, *I am so sorry.*

Sometimes, I am able to remember it wasn't all my fault. Sometimes, I am able to hear these smallest of truths: we are allowed mistakes. We are allowed a second chance.

"I DID NOT LOOK UP AGAIN"

Anne Gimm

Ten years ago, I developed a fascination with war. It began with the accounts of military women who deployed to the wars in Iraq and Afghanistan and expanded to World War II, the Civil War, and the conflicts in Korea and Vietnam. I learned that chow could be a place, a rack was something you slept in, boot camp was not the same as basic training, and moral injury was distinct from PTSD. I pored over history books while I waited in the halls of my sons' preschools, and eventually pursued my research at the Women's Memorial in Washington, D.C., at Marine Corps Base Quantico in Virginia, and in the Middle East.

I viewed this growing interest as an effort to contextualize my life: my parents had survived the Korean War before arriving in the U.S. for graduate school in the early 1960s. Like many Korean Americans, my siblings and I formed a link to our family's past through stories and fraught silences. While we were growing up, my father reminded us about his five-mile walks to school and the virtues of our ancestral lineage. My mother, by contrast, was drawn to sentimental memories of her parents and the war. She often reminisced about her brilliant father, a civil servant in the colonial Korean government, and the songs and poems that he dedicated to her. I remember listening to story after story, rapt with emotion, waiting for the catch in her throat that signaled the end. In the silence that followed, I would think about the story she wasn't telling us: one day, two agents from the North came to my mother's house and escorted her beloved father into a car. And then he disappeared.

A few years ago, I became aware of another reason for my interest in war besides my family's connection to it. I'd never talked much about 9/11, partly because it was, and still is, an uncomfortable subject for many people, and I was, and probably still am, overwhelmed by the magnitude of that day. Unlike several of my friends, I did not leave my job or find a deeper purpose in the aftermath of the attacks. Instead, I took shelter under a blanket of disquiet while I continued with my life. When my memory of 9/11 eventually returned, it revealed itself vividly and in slow motion, as traumatic events often do.

I was at the World Trade Center on the morning of September 11th, 2001. I saw the cloudless sky that I would later read about in the newspapers—its beauty only became strange in retrospect. Despite a bizarre plane accident, I sensed nothing unusual when I arrived on a high, open floor of Tower Seven. Business suits milled around me in distracted, comforting patterns while ambient news played on a flat screen TV. After my client called to postpone our meeting, I noticed something that gave me pause: the image of two smoldering towers on the large screen was identical to what I saw through the enormous window. I closed my briefcase and took the elevator to the ground floor.

The air outside was crisp with shock. I joined the ashen crowds heading north and tried to call my mother. Unable to reach her on my cell phone, I stopped at a stationary taxi to listen to a radio. While I waited, the woman standing next to me pointed at the sky. A man and a woman were hovering over a ledge of the North Tower. I could make out their features, their smooth, formal clothes. They looked like dolls gazing across Manhattan. As a voice sputtered on the radio with a news update, the woman next to me screamed. My breath quickened; I did not look up again and kept walking.

I heard the North Tower collapse before I understood that could happen. There was a long, swaying creak and a pause before the massive structure of glass and steel began to buckle under its own weight. I remember glancing over my shoulder as I ran, trapped in a scene from a comic book. When the sound gathered itself again, the tower fell swiftly, in violent cascades of debris and dust, borne by its own momentum in a headlong descent to the ground, until nothing, not even the invincible idea of it, remained.

Afterward, a burning scent spread throughout New York City that made everything taste warm and metallic, like electricity.

THERE ARE THINGS I UNDERSTAND now that I didn't know then. I think I understand the elusive authority of the silence surrounding my family's stories and 9/11. It is central to our experience of war and trauma, and it reminds us of our mysterious connection to other lives around the world and across time.

As I watch my sons grow taller than me, I sometimes wonder about my grandfather. For years, I urged my mother to find out what happened to him. Now, I no longer do. I see how the quiet protects her, like a layer of skin she may never shed. If I listen closely, maybe I will hear a song in her silence. Maybe that will be how the story ends.

"THIS WAS A BORDER CROSSING"

Scott Garson

September 30

This year, both of our babies are going to school, third grade and kindergarten. We're up early, packing lunches and such, trying to keep to our schedule. If I drive—let's say that I do—I pull to the curb across the street from the school, which is quicker than having to wait in the idling line in the circular drive. But there is a downside: my kids have to cross with the guard, then move through the crowds of grown-ups and kids and find their way into the school. It's not hard. Everybody's going to school. But I watch them—my daughter, Naomi, holding the hand of our five-year old, Levin. I lean and try to keep them in sight until they have passed through the doors.

Then I drive home.

I'm not in the classroom today. I'm grading first drafts of essays.

> *Remember that night you were already in bed*
> *Said fuck it, got up to drink with me instead*
>
> —Japandroids, "Younger Us" 7-inch
> (released on July 7th)

SEPTEMBER 30TH, we're new at our university. New in this state, new in this life. By objective measures, we're doing all right. My limited-edition collection of fiction, *American Gymnopédies*, came out in May; B's full-length ethnography, *Removing Mountains*, came out a month ago. We're, like, productive. Still, we're never relaxed. We feel not calm or efficient enough, not smooth, not gathered. Not something.

WE TRY NOT TO GIVE OURSELVES too hard a time for taking a loan and buying a hot tub and sneaking out there sometimes, even on school nights, with glasses of wine.

We're not joking, just joking, we are joking, just joking, we're not joking
—Das Racist, "hahahaha jk?"
(released on September 14th)

AT 3:28 P.M., I get a message from a fellow editor. The journal I edit, *Wigleaf*, is holding an off-site reading at the Association of Writers and Writing Programs conference in Washington D.C. in February. The fellow editor writes that we should be listed on the bookfair page soon, and a third editor responds, "Cool, man."

My relationship with these guys, though we haven't yet met, is stronger, by far, than my relationship with anyone at work, in the English Department. That's because I'm new, and because I'm non-tenure-track. I teach four sections of Composition in five hours, with a break in between for lunch. Usually, I go to McDonalds, which in that year has a location on campus, a crowded place where I will call out two older white women for racist birther talk before the 2012 election, and which I will stop frequenting soon after, when I realize how unfit I've become since leaving California.

What is it that you want to see?
I gotta go
It's in a trillion pie-ces
—No Age, "Fever Dreaming"
(released two days ago, September 28th)

WE DROVE WHEN WE LEFT the west coast for Missouri. I didn't say to B or anyone else some things I think I was thinking: how this was a border. This was a border crossing. We would be full-on adults in the Midwest. We would be doing real life.

And were we?

Did adults ponder Lady Gaga's appearance at the VMA's in a meat dress a couple of weeks ago? Did adults spend time gathering new releases from mp3 blogs?

> *Kids just let go*
> *I don't know what I'm saying*
> *Don't know what I'm saying*
> *Don't know what I'm saying*
> *Don't know what I'm saying*

—Blair, "Hello Halo"
(released on January 26th)

THERE IS SO MUCH we don't know. We don't know if B will get tenure. We don't know that my brother has heart disease. We don't know who our kids will be, or what's flying their way from the future.

One thing we do know, or sense, anyway: we're in a not bad part of life. We've got these two kids. And they're—I mean, wonderful. We read with them, hold them, talk with them. Maybe we fail in all sorts of ways, but we are okay enough to be wide, to be there for the routine joys.

OCTOBER

"JUST NERVES"

Miriam McEwen

October 2nd: In my sleep, I cling to the star-crossed lover I've been wet dreaming of for some two odd years. I am confused and scared about sex, and my subconscious mind is working hard to puzzle things out for me. The lover of my dreams changes with the hues of the night, and presently has been overtaken by a purple that is foundationally red and the color of all the wines I've yet to taste. He—for the lover evokes an earthy, bookish masculinity—does everything I tell myself I can't. He moves so I don't have to. He breathes for me. He bears down, into my poor little soul and in other ways. He is overcome with my unspeakable grief. He cries out, then dies away with the coming of their voices.

My parents would answer any one of my questions and be glad. I am their fourth daughter to go through puberty. But I'm too cold to get into it. My eyes feel swollen. I'm naked on the bed and they are in their pajamas. It doesn't matter that my body is changing or that my urges tend toward the carnal. They have to dress me for school now. And just like the rest of the county's disabled students, I have to catch the designated bus: a squat yellow death-trap that chugs along the mountain roads before dawn. It reaches my house at half past five. I'm wearing a teal Cosby sweater and the ripped jeans my daddy would've cut up for rags had I not saved them.

I am fifteen. I am perpetually furious and sensitive and artistically predisposed but undisciplined. I am in real physical pain

163

from all the sitting I do and from all the operations I've had. My sisters are either away in college or experiencing the pangs of freedom after college. But I don't really keep up with them because I get so lonely. I am selfish. I am a star student. In front of classmates and teachers I exude an eccentric Southern gentility that is mostly performative. And if I didn't have my head buried in a trashcan on this particular Friday morning—if the bitter, clear fluid that my mother calls "just nerves" would stop rising into my tightened throat—maybe I could make it down the hill in time to meet that good-for-nothing bus. But I don't want to go.

For liability reasons that are suspect at best and fictitious at worst, the school district employs someone to accompany me everywhere: to class, to the lunchroom, the bathroom, outside. Miriam's Helper is her unofficial title, and she bullies me. She has started a rumor that I urinate on myself. The already not-great school lunches are rendered inedible after she has poured three, four packets of salt over them. So, I don't eat during the day. I don't understand. She is a middle-aged woman. She has a teenager of her own. But I am different because I am troubled. I apologize to my helper regularly. The high school adminis-tration doesn't believe me when I complain that she won't let me finish a single test without challenging my answers. I am paranoid. She is making me that way. I am ugly because my beautiful hair is falling out. I think about dying. I think about sex. I want release.

The bus is waiting. My parents are at a loss. They're annoyed I'm crying again, and this time so hard snot is running into my mouth. I'll stay home today. Sleep it off. This part of my life won't last forever, you know.

"IT'S NOT A STORY I WOULD WRITE TODAY"

Rion Amilcar Scott

On this day—not October 3rd—I am revising a story I was writing on that October date ten years ago. How does one revise a story for ten years? If you were to tell me then that I would still be working on this story with a title ripped from a Biggie Smalls song—"Party & Bullshit"—I'd perhaps laugh darkly, bitterly. My worst fears confirmed. It would become obvious to me: all that I was learning in graduate school, all that I was writing, had come to absolutely nothing. The story concerns a young man who is dissatisfied with everything around him. He attends a party at a nightclub, hoping that helps him make sense of his life. He has a disastrous workday and contemplates the numerous ways his job is destroying his soul. He contemplates a relationship that he is unsure of. October 3rd was a Sunday. Sundays, these days, fill me with dread. They mean that for the next several days I will strap myself every morning into a rolling glass and metal cage to take my body to a place my heart and mind refuse to go. I am scattered to the wind, displaced. Pieces of me here and there. Rarely do I find myself united. I felt no such dread on October 3rd. I had no job to rip me apart the next day, just writing classes. I was in my parents' basement where I lived, a sanctuary I didn't know was a sanctuary, and that story kept coming. I recalled that job I had years before that drained me and I turned it into fiction, satirizing my past despair. Never again would I feel so ripped apart by a job, I thought. It was worth a laugh on the page, just as the notion of never again being destroyed by a job is worth a laugh now. Like the character, I contemplated my relationship, surely time would make coupling make sense. There was nothing I had to do to make things make sense, no actions I had to take; all I had to do was live and trust time. I realize now that that whole time—October 3rd and all its surrounding days—were a kind of Sunday. The world rushed in eventually, dreadful and dark. In roughly a year and a month, my grandmother would be gone—a sanctuary lost. People, I learned, want what they want from you and time puts nothing in order. Sundays and every other day became dreadful again, but especially Sundays. I watched pieces of me scatter and buzz about like confused gnats. I returned to "Party & Bullshit" frequently, changing a sentence here, deciding it's brilliant and then condemning it as a hack job, sending it out for publication and collecting rejection after rejection. The manuscript that the story was initially a part of, I watched it become a bloated mess and one day it spontaneously combusted, metaphorically, of course. I salvaged "Party & Bullshit" for some reason, perhaps to hold on to that October 3rd feeling. That time, like all times, is gone though. I look at the sentences now and try as I revise to honor the twenty-seven-year-old who wrote them. Many of the things that mattered to him, don't matter to me now and so many things should have mattered to him. It's not a story I would write today, but one I would revise, forever if I have to from Sunday to Sunday, with the faith that I can recast ten years of memories into a story I can live with.

"YOU COME BY IT HONESTLY"

Cassidy McCants

> *Time is the school in which we learn,*
> *time is the fire in which we burn.*
>
> —Delmore Schwartz

Birthdays can feel complicated, but it's the day after that always gets me.

Early October, back in Tulsa after a brief internship in the magical and unaffordable San Francisco, I fled home once again to see a 1960s adaptation of Chekhov's *The Seagull*. The play, adapted and directed by my aunt Laurie, was put on by the Bloomsburg Theatre Ensemble, which she co-founded in 1978.

The small college town was at peak charm, its historic downtown bustling with locals and students in the early-fall cold. We celebrated after the show at her 1900 red-brick Victorian home, tchotchkes and art from all over the world lining the walls. We shared beer (kept cold in "Allah's freezer," her large screened-in porch), wine, snacks, and I drank in the way my aunt had built her life not only to support and celebrate art but to *be* art itself. The firepit in the backyard and Tom Waits' "Hold On" and "Come on Up to the House" kept us warm. I'd fly home the next day, my twenty-fourth birthday. I felt alive and ready to build something a fraction as beautiful as this for myself.

Two days later, I'm back home, crying in my dad's truck. "Is it even [the day after] your birthday if you don't cry?" my friend Hannah would say. My dad, brother, and I had gone to see Beck at what was then called the Brady Theater, since renamed the Tulsa Theater, brought on by W. Tate Brady's association with the KKK. Maybe it was "Lost Cause" that set me off. That's a cryable song.

Though I was aiming to be a fiction writer—that is, I hadn't written a thing in the year and a half since finishing undergrad—the artist community I'd found in Tulsa was the musicians. They were visible, varied, constantly working, and their art was accessible in a way short stories never could be again, or so it felt. I was making a habit of spending every night out on the town, trying to make my life art, trying to be a good (though broke) arts patron, and looking for love in the late-night fuzziness, the faint, torch-like glow of cellar bars and pubs.

I think the tears were more *Why am I like this?* than anything. Seeking a life of passion and art meant constantly facing the highs and the lows, and I never could put into words what would send me to tears on these late nights. Something like *It's all so great and it's all so awful*, a basic idea, or two truths I am more than capable of holding, most of the time, in the light of day. To be so sensitive feels juvenile, silly, the same way the pull to be an artist can feel frivolous, self-important. "You come by it honestly," my dad said that night, crying with me. My mom would say the same.

Fast-forward two years and we see a recurring theme: I'm driving my dad's truck because my first model year Honda Fit has finally pooped out on me. A truck with a Bernie sticker, an "I stand with Standing Rock" sticker, and Grateful Dead dancing bear decals. "Be careful driving through Harrison," he'd tell me. For this particular drive, though, Tulsa to Tecumseh, I could course just north of the town of thirteen thousand, a town that at that time had a billboard on the main stretch of 412: "Anti-racist is a code word for anti-white." A chilling message presumably funded by the KKK.

I am hungover. I take a photo of myself halfway through the four-hour drive to see how bad I really look. Typically baby-faced, today my twenty-six years (as of yesterday) look like at least thirty-five. My head pounds, and I break down crying every half hour on the road. I'm afraid I have a concussion. I focus on two or three songs this trip, playing them over and over until I can sing one adequately all the way through—no tears, no quivers, no bubbles in the throat or forgotten lyrics. One was "Ripple," a favorite of my dad's, one that got closer to describing the idea of God than any other he'd known. He's an atheist; I didn't question this.

Road trips create, for me, a space and time for indulging both melancholy and cheer, frustration and gratitude. An opportunity to feel all those big feelings, to celebrate even the darkest ones. This drive to Tecumseh might have come at a perfect time, then, because mere hours ago I was losing myself to one of those drunken, sad stupors. I had walked the streets of Tulsa crying. I had, after falling in my bathroom, hit my head repeatedly on the side of my bathtub, when I made it home in the middle of the night. The nice woman on the other side of the duplex must have been either scared or angry; maybe she even banged on the walls to stop me, to scold me.

It was my birthday, after all. I thought I'd found the love I was looking for, but I was grappling with the fact that the person I loved had admitted to living a double life. Now this phrasing seems hilarious to me, a glamorized portrayal of maintaining two almost-relationships in two different cities. As does the way he told me in a session with his therapist—no, wait, he didn't even tell *me*, he told the therapist while I was sitting there. My response? Over the next few weeks, I alternated between comforting him—I know, I know—and berating him. Maybe I'd grown too accustomed, even attached, to the highs and lows in this life I'd sought out for myself.

The good news, though, is I was heading for a writing retreat. Soon I would be with friends from my MFA program who found it hard to believe I would behave the way I described, who maybe even thought I was embellishing when I said I thought

I had a concussion from the many falls the night before. After a quick ER trip to reassure myself I wasn't brain-bleeding to the point of death, I was able to be present for the magic of true community. We were all choosing this way of life, a way of life that felt, to me, difficult to describe to outsiders.

Now I am actually nearing thirty-five, and my grays and fine lines show it. I have that fiction degree (from a tiny town in Vermont, not unlike my aunt's idyllic Pennsylvania town), a reminder that it doesn't have to feel frivolous or impractical to prioritize an artistic life, even when—or especially when—white supremacists are still spewing hate on small-town billboards. What I think has happened is I've learned to stop questioning myself so much. Maybe, simply, some people are built this way, and some are not. It takes all kinds, and the only thing I've ever felt good at or felt like I had to offer was words on the page, so I guess I have to just roll with it. In the past few years my life has shaped up into a fairly stable one: I have a practical day job, I share a beautiful and loving home with my partner, and I've just learned I'm pregnant. My body feels abuzz with not just creation but creativity and possibility, and I both dread and look forward to the day when I get to tell my crying child, *You come by it honestly.*

"I DID NOT KNOW THERE WOULD BE YOU"

JJ Rushing

October 10

I did not know
there would be
You
new and mighty
bright as a full moon

I did not know
You
would be born
and I reborn at forty-two

I did not know
your father would let go of my hand
and I would find my feet
the steel of
You
fusing to my spine

I did not know
I would go this alone
broken hearted and full hearted

I did not know
You
would be
all my reasons

Ten years on and
You
are here
wise and driven

and I am younger now
new and mighty
bright as a full moon

"WHERE THE RIVERS, MOUNTAINS, AND OCEAN CONVERGE"

Adam Sawyer

October 18th was a restful day and the innocuous filling in a substantial life events sandwich. Just two days prior, I had submitted the final manuscript of my first hiking guidebook. What I didn't know at the time, was that many more would follow. Two days after the 18th, I would try heroin for the first time. Unfortunately for me, that would not be an isolated occurrence, either.

I became addicted to opiates the first time when I was in the military and prescribed opiate painkillers for my headache—GI Aspirin, they were called at the time, and I had a hell of a time with them. They eventually resulted in a felony conviction, the loss of my military career, and a one-year prison sentence. Fast forward to Portland, Oregon, almost a decade later.

I was hanging out with some friends and celebrating the completion of my book when I was offered heroin. I initially scoffed and was actually kind of offended since the person doing the offering was well aware of my past. I emphatically declined. But about thirty minutes later and after ten years clean, I tracked them down and was soon huddled in a bathroom corner smoking black tar heroin off a sheet of tin foil.

It was around this same time that I began dating a wonderful woman who was a single mother of two boys. As love was blossoming, my usage was entering full bloom as well. Living on love and delightfully smitten, I was simultaneously, and quite nonchalantly, entering into a steady two-year downward spiral.

My girlfriend caught me or found questionable paraphernalia in my possession a few times over the course of our relationship, and was, needless to say, unimpressed. I would tell her that I only did it occasionally, but if it made her uncomfortable, I would stop. Which it did, and which I did not. Then she caught me smoking H in the bathroom of her two-bedroom apartment one morning while the kids were eating breakfast. That did it for her and she quite justifiably had to let me go. Additionally, the career I had worked so hard to manifest was being actively flushed down the toilet. Shortly thereafter, I entered a detox facility.

After getting clean, I moved into a friend's house and began what I knew from experience would be a painfully slow process. The endorphin receptors that heroin destroys can eventually be repaired. Luckily, one of the things that helps the process along is fresh air and exercise. The outdoors of Oregon is what inspired me to become a writer in the first place. Before losing my way two years prior, hiking had been my drug of choice. It would become a critical component in returning to health. But I did eventually make it to the other side of that battle. However, this time it was facilitated by the outdoors and not the inside of a prison cell.

While I was nursing my career and myself back to health, I would find love again. Actually, the love of my life. I met Kara through a mutual friend the year prior but we were both on different paths at the time. We all met for dinner and drinks one night, and not long after that Kara asked if I would be interested in a "semi-platonic hang out." Four days later, I would go back to my own home for the evening to prove to myself that I could. That was the last time I would go to a "home" that wasn't where she was.

Our chemistry was insane across the board. We didn't just fall in love, we were shot into it out of a cannon. After living together for a few years in Portland, for a variety of reasons we made our move out to the country. An off-the-grid-home on five acres in the woods of Washington.

By our third year we had settled into our groove. Having discovered the hows and whys of off-grid living, we were kind of killing it. I try not to say this very often and never in mixed company, but the pandemic brought out the full shine on us and our chosen situation.

It was the happiest that either one of us had ever been. Ever. I had only hoped for a life as fulfilling and roundly gratifying as this. All needs perfectly met. All wants exquisitely satiated. What else could a sentient being ever desire from existence? Other than its continuance. Unfortunately, it did not continue.

In the early morning hours of February 25th, 2022, what is believed to have been an electrical malfunction triggered a fire at our home in the woods. I was safely away for work, but the fire escalated so quickly and with such intensity, that both Kara and our cat Lela were unable to escape, and perished in the blaze. By the time it was extinguished later that morning, most of the home and its belongings were gone, as well.

For the entirety of my adult life, I have been a purposeful nomad. "Home" was both a technicality and an abstract. Until I met a person who was, for me, the manifestation of the concept. As much as I loved our place in the woods, as much as it was my all-time favorite mailing address, the home I lost that day was Kara.

Shortly thereafter, a travel industry friend and owner of the Old Wheeler Hotel on the Oregon coast allowed me to move in and stay until I could find a place to land. Over the course of the next year and a half, I spent as much time in nature as possible to grieve, heal, and find much-needed perspectives.

Beyond those things, I have found great inspiration here as well. The Oregon coast is regularly battered by wind, rain, and surf. It absorbs some of the most brutal onslaughts that the elements have to offer with reliable, historic consistency. And as long as there have been human memories to detail such things, it has exuded an uncommon beauty and resilience in the face of it all. This place is home to some of the most wondrous and life-affirming landscapes I've ever laid eyes on. Perhaps not despite what it goes through, but because of it.

I would wind up calling the small town of Wheeler home for eight months before finally moving into a more permanent residence. Still on the coast, about a half-hour down the road near the town of Tillamook. At this juncture in my life, it feels somewhere between compelling and critical to be near the elk and the salmon. Where the rivers, mountains, and ocean converge. Where my favorite trees of fragrant needles and flat leaves connect the sand to the soil. Here there is life and abundance that is impossible not to be touched or influenced by. I find beauty, inspiration, meaning, and purpose every day here. It's where I belong, for now, anyway.

Among the many things that Mother Nature has taught me, it's that things take time—their own time. Additionally, not all of her cycles are equal, easily understood, or by human empathetic assessment, remotely fair. I've learned to be okay with that. I kind of have to be. It's been a somewhat recent development, but I can honestly say that I am ready to continue the journey forward with a heart that is wide open to whatever lies ahead in this life.

We kind of have to be.

"BANGTASTIC"

Christopher Gonzolez

I like to think the five of us drove to the 7 Floors of Hell together, by which I mean J drove her father's car and I sat on the passenger side, running my mouth, talking shit. That's accurate no matter the year, my shit-talking at someone else's side.

On October 31st, I wanna say we stopped for dinner at Steak 'n Shake first, but that's likely a false memory, too. Maybe it was actually the Applebee's across the street, or the Taco Bell across from that. Any restaurant in Steelyard Commons, which was named for the hub of metallurgical and scrap plants towering over the Cuyahoga River, in its deep backyard. I was switching between glasses and contact lenses around this time so, depending on the night, when I looked up at the smokestacks, I'd either see clear flames or a kaleidoscope of blues and oranges, this constant reminder that I could never quite settle into my surroundings.

I would be shocked if we didn't smoke Black & Milds in the parking lot that night, so I'll say it's true. In my five-day tenure of being eighteen, I must have made at least three trips to the gas station after school to pick up a pack. We always bought wine-flavored because they allegedly tasted the best, though all I remember is a dulled funk that stuck to my throat and made me gag. H taught me how to freak them while waiting for the bus home; I never managed to do it on my own.

But, okay, for sure, this was around the time we started using "bangtastic" to describe anyone we found attractive, regardless of their gender. Waiting in line for the first haunted house, we whispered to each other that he was bangtastic and she was bangtastic. A true jackpot was seeing a couple, their hands intertwined, and deciding that, objectively, they were both bangtastic. I can't remember who started it, either J or I did, but it caught on quickly. I should be clear: we didn't cat-call anyone. We always said it in whispers, and maybe that's also bad, but at the time it felt like I was pulling off a heist, getting to call another guy cute without saying the words out loud. Without being sincere about my own fragile desires. My internal monologue was a drawn-out pendulum swing between straight and gay because discourse around the very notion of bisexual boys in high school was so toxic it didn't really exist.

(I wanna say I was a good friend to my friends, most of whom were girls and much more unapologetic about how they moved through the world. I was the only dude in the group, which wasn't a problem and should never be a problem, but there were times I'd build up a wall to hide from being seen as too soft or too emotional, being seen as myself. Maybe in the last four years I've started to see light penetrate the cracks of that wall, or at least I hope so.)

I can't leave out the fact that, at school, my friends and I had collectively developed crushes on a number of teachers, because they were white and kind to us. They seemed so much older, too, and put together (well, except for the one), but now I'm about three years younger than they were at the time and I understand their lives must have been in shambles. Dear, God. How could they not have been? Embarrassingly, I pined hard for them. For our English teacher who wore flowy dresses, the finance teacher who launched insults with a smirk, our algebra teacher with ginger sideburns, and my AP chemistry teacher who looked like a young John Goodman. He taught us jack-shit about chemistry, but through him I learned that one could, in fact, exist as fat and attractive and funny and confident.

I could have loved myself more. But I didn't know that kindness wasn't only for others.

I WISH I COULD TELL YOU MORE about the actual haunted houses. Their layouts and themes. The number of blood stains. If we met a man with a loud chainsaw. If house seven was as scary as the first. Does anything beat the first? I can't say for sure, trust me. Certainly, it's scarier going through it than to look back on it.

NOVEMBER

"OUR FUTURE IS AT OUR MOUTH"

Elizabeth Austin

Boa constrictors swallow their prey whole, without chewing it. After that they are not able to move, and they sleep through the six months that they need for digestion.

—*The Little Prince*, Antoine de Saint-Exupéry

November 6

When my daughter swallowed the last of the pills that saved her life, my son cheered. I held my thumb over the "record" button on my phone, documenting the moment, saving it forever. I watched it hundreds of times in the months after, each time considering how strange it feels to be on the other side of something that for so long took up all the available space in our lives. There was the before cancer, and now there is the after, and in the middle a lump the size of an elephant too large to comprehend.

A decade earlier, when my kids were in their early reading years, I tried to read *The Little Prince* to them in the original French. I hoped they'd pick some of the language up. *Look*, I tried to engage them, *The fox! The stars! Look at le petit prince, our tiny hero!* They looked away, bored, and reached for a Dr. Seuss. *Fox in socks on Knox in box!* they chimed as I raced my way through tongue twisters, my mind still among the stars.

The closest we'd come to cancer was St. Jude's billboards on the highway and viral social media videos. I watched window washers dressed up as superheroes waving at kids through huge panels of hospital glass and thought, *How sweet.* Then we were on the other side of the window and all I could think about was throwing a rock through it. I didn't know how to be a cancer family before we were one, and I spent the early part of my daughter's cancer years always trying to shed that skin. *This isn't us,* I'd repeat to myself while my kid puked yellow bile into a bedpan. *We're just visiting.* Eventually we'd return to our normal life.

Do you remember this? I asked, while my daughter's body shivered against my own. *The little boy traveling through outer space?* I'd pulled the book from my shelf on our way out the door, not thinking about much beyond getting to the hospital. She shrugged, her fever climbing, the antibiotics making her eyelids heavy. *Read it to me anyway,* she said, tipping her head into my chest, and I started. *Lorsque j'avais six ans j'ai vu, une fois, une magnifique image, dans un livre sur la forêt vierge qui s'appelait Histoires vécues. Ça représentait un serpent boa qui avalait un fauve. Voilà la copie du dessin.*

I read her the story of the volcanoes and the sheep hiding inside the box, the prince's lost planet and the rose that always needed more no matter how much he gave. I read until the nurses came in whispering their goodnights. My eyes traced the strange words in the low lights of the vital sign monitors, a story I knew as well as I knew our own. *Look,* I whispered into my daughter's hair, *the fox, the stars. Look at our tiny hero.*

Years later, while my daughter made her last dose of chemo disappear in a swallow of red Gatorade, I thought about the boa constrictor in *The Little Prince*—the one that swallowed the elephant. Our life seemed to stretch across a page in time like the skinny body of the snake. Those nights when I would read to my kids in hopeful French trails like a tail behind us. Our future is at our mouth, getting smaller with every bite, and there is the elephant in the middle—cancer, taking up so much space I can't believe we're still able to breathe around it. We'd need to sleep for six months just to digest it all.

I can tick ten marks on the line of our lives, one for every November 6th we've survived. One year, I am painting my daughter's face like Wonder Woman, the yellow tiara crooked, the red center jewel skewed. In another she is running down the hill of my mother's front yard chasing something just outside the frame of my mind. Then there are gurneys, bags of blood, thick yellow fluids hanging from hospital poles. For years she is bald, a feeding tube trailing from her right nostril, hanging over her ear like a vine. Then she tips her head to the sky and swallows, and it's over so fast I almost want it back.

I'm not ready, I think, *for what comes after.*

"I THINK I COULD BECOME MYSELF HERE"

Kelle Groom

Ten years ago on November 10th, I lived on the top floor of the painter Hans Hofmann's house in the West End of Provincetown, MA. It had been Hofmann's painting studio, overlooking Cape Cod Bay. I'd been traveling for over two years on writing residencies and teaching, mostly living in places I'd never been, where I knew no one. But that summer I'd returned to the Cape which I had always considered home. My mother's family had always lived on the mid-Cape, my father had gone there when he was sixteen and made it his home. I'd spend my early childhood there, all summers. Now, I'd left my belongings behind in a storage unit in Florida and was thinking and writing about home. Where is it? What is it?

Provincetown is the Outer Cape, land's end; a two-mile wide sandbar seventy-five miles out to sea. As far as you can go. In September, I'd been between residencies, and friends had given me their place in the Hofmann house. For the first time, I was without a full-time job and trying to make a life as a writer.

On November 10th, I left the white curtained alcove enclosing the bed, made coffee. Broke and struggling, with no income until my next residency in January at James Merrill's House in CT. On the counter, I'd made a pyramid of Progresso soup cans (on sale $1 each) and could have one per day. The soup, along with oatmeal, noodles, and occasionally eating at the

186

Provincetown Soup Kitchen was my entire diet. I lost a lot of weight but found that heating food to a very hot temp made it more filling.

I don't know that in eight days, I'll receive a phone call from the National Endowment for the Arts telling me I've been awarded a $25,000 Fellowship in Prose.

It was thirty-nine degrees. I walked up to the widow's walk at the top of the house. In the cold air, I was surrounded by the ocean. Light silver, overcast, but at the horizon a soft yellow, and peach/pink reflected in the middle of the bay, rippling.

I'd been taking photographs since I started traveling, documenting each place: Washington, D.C.; Las Vegas, Lake Tahoe, Wyoming, the Santa Cruz Mountains, the summer in Wellfleet, MA; and now Provincetown. Gray peaked roofs behind me. I wore a navy scarf, sweater, and black coat with gray fleece.

My family's only home on the Cape had sold in September. My 1997 green Jeep was in the broken shell drive outside. I found warm enough clothes to bike to the ocean. The road outside the house under construction, tar globular and pebbly, but dry enough to bike on.

Sunday. Streets empty. Right turn toward the marsh and the Province Lands, Cape Cod National Seashore. Marsh on my left now opened up with light and water. Then the empty beach parking lot I turned into, biked across. The ocean blue-black. Opaque. Cement-like with low waves. But the white clouds had a delicate pink below. I'd told my downstairs neighbor that I wanted to bike to the beach this winter. He'd said, "You need to get hardier." I'd added a black wool hat, fleece leggings. Low tide, I crossed the gully between beach and sandbar, so that I walked right beside the water.

In November the sun sets at 4:30 p.m., darkness a blanket, town shut down. In photos of this day, the sun on my face was the golden light before sunset. Otherworldly. Transforming the dunes and me in luminescence. So warm it was like a hand. My eyes closed. White foam of the waves blazing. I was (am) trying to learn how to live with uncertainty. How to stay in the day. I'd walked out as far as I could. I had to be aware of the tide, as it came in fast. If I were too far out when it came in, I could be trapped on the sandbar for six hours. Until the tide changed. In November, there's no way to cross the body of water between the sandbar and the beach. You'd freeze.

The ocean turned blacker. Sky darkening except for yellow light like an annunciation far out to sea, with an oval of orange in it. I wrote to my friend Terry in Florida, "I think I could become myself here." It was so quiet, I could pay attention to everything.

I stayed until the ocean was black, and a hole opened up in the center of the now dark sky—a white light like a giant flashlight. One seagull flew by.

I'll bike home before dark. Cook noodles to make soup. My friends had lots of spices in their cupboard. On another day, I'd walk to my friend Larry's fine art and antiques shop. Sit by the front door in his very comfortable chair. Relax in the warmth. Larry would take out piece after piece, telling me about it, teaching. I especially loved his collection of ruby glass photographs. Looking close to see the faces inside. Winter is slow in Provincetown, and it seemed there was always time to talk and listen and pay attention.

That November would be my first Thanksgiving in Provincetown, and Larry will order all my favorite foods from the amazing health food store in town (now gone). We'll eat at a table in his tiny condo overlooking the bay. And then this will become our tradition, to always have Thanksgiving together.

But on November 10, 2013, that was still ahead—the NEA Fellowship, my growing friendship with Larry, my eventual return to Provincetown in 2015 to live and work for seven years. And the book of these years of traveling, *HOW TO LIVE: A Memoir in Essays*, published October 2023, by Tupelo Press.

On that day, I was calmed and grateful for my freedom, the time and space—water, light, dunes, friendship, recovery meetings, gift of a home—all helping me learn how to live.

"IN THE DECADE SINCE MY ESSAY WAS PUBLISHED"

Patrick Madden

In which the essayist returns to Montevideo, and to his decade-old essay, to update and to reconsider, perhaps to say goodbye.

November 12

When last we met, exactly ten years ago, I was holding forth on technological innovations to improve the public transportation system of Montevideo. You were patiently reading along, perhaps half-distracted, wondering about the point of my musings, humoring me, maybe out of obligation, maybe out of boredom. I have good news to report. In the decade since my essay was published, the very thing I was wishing for has come to pass. At least partially. You can now download the STM (Sistema de Transporte Metropolitano) Montevideo app and use it to locate bus stops and routes, to track when the next bus will arrive, and to map out the most efficient way to your destination. The app will not tell you, however, how likely you are to find a seat, or whether you'll have to stand. I remain hopeful (seeing how Google maps offers such user-provided data both live and historical), but for the time being, I'll be happy with what I get.

I have bad news, too. As luck would have it, I'm once again (and unexpectedly) in Montevideo, which I love, but for a reason I don't. My mother-in-law has been sick, is now confined to bed, and likely will not recover. We don't know. I try to remain hopeful, but there's a nagging part of me that understands my hope to be unfounded and foolish. She was sent home from the hospital two days before Karina and I arrived, and while nobody has quite pronounced the word "hospice," the general sense seems to be that her care is purely palliative. The doctors who visit are gentle and kind, but their bearing seems to convey their belief that there's no return from where she's at.

In revisiting my old essay here, I had intended to write not about bus-tracking technology, nor about my mother-in-law's decline, but about the fact that ten years ago, before I left Uruguay to return to Utah but after I wrote my Dispatch from Montevideo, I finally (and unexpectedly) met with Tathi and Rafa, the two lovers whose spat led the latter to spray paint his sloppy apologies on the whitewashed walls along the 174 bus route down Bulevar Aparicio Saravia

> *Tathi, I love you*
> *Forgive me*

leading me to wonder about the characters involved and their backstory, to seek them out, to discover certain small details and third-person reports; but, by the time of writing, I had failed to make contact. I think I had intended, after I'd finally talked with them, to post a follow up, rife with details about what they told me when we spoke, eagerly suggesting the hopeful belief that maybe we *can* connect with one another, if we take the time to sit and listen, and forgive.

All that's gone now. My memory's a near blank, and I find only the sparsest of notes in my files:

> *Tathi*
> *18 recién, 3 años juntos, 5 años después*
> *orange house, taller de motos*

I've retained almost nothing else of our conversation. I recall that we met at a plaza in Peñarol; we sat on a low brick wall, or they did, and I sat facing them, or stood, or... I call it a "brick" wall for the sake of the sentence, but perhaps it was made of cinder block with a concrete top. Or maybe stone. Of the two young people I recall only generalities: they were soft-spoken, gentle, a bit confused by my interest, unsure of my purposes, yet willing to share their story, perhaps a bit guardedly. I may have let them believe that I was the kind of writer they were imagining, the kind who has lots of readers, motivated by more than personal obligations or boredom. I surely never suggested, nor thought, that I would leave the interview unrecorded and unremarked for a decade.

(Perhaps, I let myself believe now, spurred by the word that came to me unbidden just above, I recorded the audio on my phone. This is the kind of thing I would have done. I'd also have left the file untranscribed, forgotten about it, and thrown it away with my device when it became outdated.)

I could imagine for you here a believable recreation of our discussion, and you'd be none the wiser, you might even find the exchange inspiring if I did it right, but I'm more interested in the kind of honesty that admits (as in "allows") my nearly utter loss, my general lean into oblivion. I can recall almost nothing of my interlocutors' habits and features, their tone of voice, their examples and explanations. If we stood waiting at the same bus stop today, I would not recognize them. They had been dating, yes. Rafa had done something boneheaded but not life-threatening. Late one night (I feel confident that it was night), perhaps penitent and drunken (less confident), he schemed to humble himself publicly, set out with a can of black spray paint, expressed his remorse along the walls of the neighborhood. "And did it work?" I asked. "A little," Tathi said. She was inclined to forgive the poor idiot, but not yet ready to get back together with him. Or maybe they were back together. Maybe they'd been back together briefly but not anymore. Whatever the current situation, Rafa now expressed an additional regret, for having defaced his neighbors' property, especially because he did so in a way so easy to trace back to him. Before we parted, I fulfilled a promise I'd made to his neighbor Hilda and asked Rafa to get a bucket of paint to restore her wall to its undefiled state. He said he would.

And maybe he did. I can't remember if it happened soon or a long time after, but I've returned to Montevideo for family visits and for research many times since that nearly forgotten conversation, and I can confirm that the graffiti has been covered up. I've ridden the route just today, in fact, to find that I can no longer recognize the several places that once spoke this young man's wish for things to be different.

So I return to the home where my mother-in-law lies pained and unmoving in a room down the hall as I write my essay, hoping to share of myself, my experiences and my musings, to connect, to move you in some small way beyond your boredom. Every now and then she cries out. Sometimes she wants water; sometimes relief. Sometimes her intentions are not clear. She tells her children to turn off the lights that are already off, or to kick down the door to let in more light, or air, or something she cannot articulate. Once, in apparent clarity, she called out for her husband of five decades, who died six months ago, and said she wanted to go with him but didn't know how to get there. On good days, she speaks to us, asking for what she needs. I try to help, but I often feel like I'm in the way. Sometimes, when there's no pressing need to feed her or move her, when no one else is in the room, I appear with a smile on my face, trying to offer words of encouragement or ask her what she needs, speaking loudly because she no longer wears her hearing aids. "Teresa," I say, "Mamá. ¿En qué te puedo ayudar?" Mostly her answer is silence. Although we've had so many laughs and heartfelt conversations over the decades, as well as some disagreements, now, in this strange, uncomfortable place where she's arrived, it seems like the best thing to do is hold her hand, sit quietly, and remember.

"SITTING IN A DIM HALLWAY, WAITING FOR A CONNECTION"

Rima Rantisi

November 20th, I sat in the hallway outside my apartment on the fifth floor where I could catch the internet signal from my third-floor neighbors. They had given me the password, because they treated me like family, and having just started my third year in Beirut, I still did not know how to do official things like get a phone line.

I told Kathryn, who was in Chicago, in a feverish all-small-caps message that I couldn't Skype her because I was in the hallway and if my crazy neighbor heard my echoey voice slide under her door, past her shrine to all the Christian saints, I'd get a voice-whipping, and I was scared of her. The first day I had moved into that apartment, she had stood at her doorway as I worked on my computer, peering at me from across the hallway, her face slick with Botox, her cigarette smoke swirling around her like a scream.

"Where are you getting the internet from?" she asked.

Without hesitation, I smiled cheekily and said, "You!" even though I had just told myself, *Don't tell her!* The next day, of course, the net was cut.

Mona's kids were in the U.S., one of whom, according to her, was a big-shot Physics professor who never called. Like many people living in Beirut, who survived the war, whose kids had immigrated, who lived precariously in an old-rent building, her nerves were shot. She rarely left her house, but when she did, she would change out of her pajamas, blow-dry her hair, put on full make-up and a miniskirt and would head, usually, to the grocery store. If she heard the click of my door opening in the morning, she would open hers and invite me in to read dream interpretations and coffee cups. She'd light a Marlboro red, offer me one, and pull the dream book out from under her chair cushion. I would read her coffee cup; she would read me the dream book.

What Mona didn't know was that on my own time, I was regularly reading Astrologyzone.com and asking the goddesses of the tarot for answers. Like her, tapping into my future meant something to look forward to. I had just started a new decade, thirty. The specter of a future was upon me, real life could begin at any time. It was the last decade I would be young, and it was when, so I was told, I would know more about myself than ever. I was intent on, as they say, making something of myself. As if myself wasn't a thing yet.

As if always sitting in a dim hallway, waiting for a connection.

At forty, life suddenly rolled in from my thirties, which started with running a marathon because I wanted to feel powerful and that I could survive my most recent breakup. I started a blog and a journal and later got another writing degree because I wanted to be a writer. I took a guy seriously and married him and had a baby and started a family because it felt right. I put concerted efforts into my friendships because some were far and some were new, and I needed them. I sent my nephews books over the years because I wanted them to love reading. I traveled to more and more countries because it's what I always wanted to do. I spent long summers with my family because I wanted to remain close to them and be home. I became politically active because I was desperate for a change in the country. I learned to count to three before speaking because I didn't want to give myself away all the time.

At forty, I am in the future. I write from my office at home, where I live with my family and always have an internet connection from the comfort of my couch. My body is beat. I am taking a break from the outside world, where Lebanon has been in the midst of a revolution for exactly a month. It's been more than forty years of the same warlords in power and the rot festering in its deep cracks has been splayed out. The most repeated phrase of the past month has been, "There is no turning back." There is a people's power on the street that has been building itself for years. The change seems sudden, but it was all those years that mattered. And what about the future of the revolution? Who knows, but it feels like it's now.

"I AM ASIAN BEN BUTTON"

Jennifer Pun

It's November 21st, and I am rushing through LAX—it's the third time in my life I've visited the City of Angels. I zig zag past a family pulling large suitcases wrapped in plastic, a mother with a baby strapped to her chest, a group of flight attendants, men in army fatigues, Harrison Ford? (I do a double take, it's not). I'm nearing the exit, but I still have to find the taxi stand and get to my girlfriend Tricia's wedding before it starts.

At thirty-three, I am recently divorced, having traded in the suburban life hosting barbeques and tending koi ponds for a downtown Victorian with four roommates and a severely overweight cat; I took up climbing, longboarding and a short stint trying to learn to play the guitar; I got bangs and my nose pierced. The movie *The Curious Case of Benjamin Button* (based on F. Scott Fitzgerald's short story) —about an old man who grows young—had just premiered. I am Asian Ben Button, living life backwards, partying like I am back in college, except now I have disposable income.

The cab pulls up to the entrance of the wedding venue–an atrium with rows of bamboo chairs and deep red roses and a breeze that hints of the Pacific. Tricia floats down the aisle dressed in white with ruby accents. She and I are the same age, both Leos, and yet she is a woman surer of herself than I will ever be. Married, suburban homeowner me is a person I no longer relate to. I am rewinding in time to my early twenties where memories are made with lemon drops and Jell-O shots.

When the ceremony ends, I work my way to my assigned seat. A man sits beside me. He's wearing a dark navy suit and striped, yellow tie and introduces himself as Chris. "Friend of the bride?" I ask. He nods. "Me too," I say.

I'll spend the next five years traveling back and forth from Toronto to L.A. to see Chris. I'll learn in the process that we hold our pens the same way—like a claw; we both share a perverse love of spreadsheets and have terrible memories. He watches movies in silence while I yell at the TV. Chris never asks me to grow up. He accepts my arrested development. Travel is my number one priority; I respond to the idea of settling down with, "Sometime, maybe."

Eventually, I will become pregnant. My body will change in preparation for the baby's arrival while my mind grapples with the knowledge that another life chapter is closing. For the second time, I'll say "I do," and I'll move south of the 49th parallel. I'll give birth to our son. He too will hold his pen like a claw.

It's summer 2019. We're at our friend's wedding in northern Ontario. It's the first time in months Chris and I have been together sans child. Something clicks and I turn to him and say, "We've known each other for nine years?" "Ten," he says. Time is not on our side. "Our thirties were fun," I say. He knows me too well—my half-cocked smile and far off stare as I recall our early days of dating with the same fondness I once had for my twenties. "You're Benjamin Buttoning again," he says. I've lost the nose ring, but I still have the bangs. And I wonder if that feeling of wanting to go backwards will ever pass—of reliving the last decade and thinking those years were the best.

Today, our five-year-old wants to be older. "Six is so far away," he says. Chris tells him, "You will never be as young as you are right now, so enjoy it." I glance at our son; our urban family of three; and think: we will never be as young as we are right now. Or right now. Or right now. So, enjoy it.

I'll try to remember that.

"IT'S A SATURDAY—
PAUL WALKER IS DEAD"

Samuel Gilpin

November 30

it's a saturday—Paul Walker is dead
i catch a flight from pdx to slc
i do not know in a month i'll have
one of my episodes
having to leave it all again

but what is behind that door?
above temple square, capital hill
apricot ave, the ward close by
alone in that house
renting that house from that woman
who lost her son at sea, a sad
sad woman
in that basement behind that door
a little child's bed made up
a little child's room
full of dolls and polka dot
dresses and sad letters to a son
that lagging wind, that half-light

i remember one night

hearing your voice over the phone
thinking your voice
sounded strange

when the weather turned and you couldn't get out of bed
and that oppressive gray scale claiming everything again and
going over everything again and you're twenty-three or twenty
four years old teaching
at grad school and within that first semester you're gone
again and starting over again and falling into that pattern that
doggedly pursues you

i had quit smoking and chewing tobacco surprisingly
i chewed nicorette non-stop
N. is still there
we talked always of being poets and yogis
and she came to me and she cried about her drinking
i still pay her bills every month

and you don't believe in ghosts or really anything about
the spiritual but those old mormon houses are full of old sad-
nesses and dolls and old dresses and there are rooms in those
sad basements that stay locked and there is that door that you
question and feel when you walk into that house and you're
told that you can never go through that locked door and into
that old basement and you always hear those scratches and little
movements in the morning's half-light and you stare at that
door in your mirrors reflection as you shave in the morning

it's a saturday—Paul Walker is dead

DECEMBER

"WE FEEL SAFER"

Alex Myers

December 1st: It is a few weeks away from our seven-year wedding anniversary and Ilona and I are joking about what we'll do (we never do anything) to celebrate it. We're joking about the so-called "seven-year itch." Neither of us feel it.

But mostly we're talking about getting married. Again. To each other.

We are laughing about this in the living room of our apartment in a boys' dorm on the campus of an Episcopal School in Rhode Island. We are responsible for the thirty-four boys who live here; it is a red brick box of a dorm; it is a campus in every way steeped in tradition and old-school values. Values like marriage; to live in the dorm with your partner, you must be a married couple.

The fire in our fireplace is lit. The cats are stretched out in front of it. We have mugs of herbal tea and are playing a board game—Carcassonne—on the floor, just outside the ring of firelight. One cat's tail twitches, almost knocking over the pieces.

We are a married couple, but we need to get married again. The laws are wreaking havoc on our state of matrimony. It's complicated as a transgender guy, but essentially, the same sex civil union we got seven years ago in Vermont has been rendered null by a change in my birth certificate and a change in Vermont's law to recognize same sex marriage, and not just civil unions.

So, we are laughing about our un-marriage, about suddenly living in a state of sin according to our school, about our cozy life as a couple, about the waving cat tail that has just obliterated our board game.

It takes us a while to get the paperwork together, but we eventually do, returning to Vermont for another round of wedding vows, a new set of paperwork. It feels excessive, to have to do this again. It feels strange to have all these legal declarations; I am now male, we are now married, these things can be changed by powers far beyond us.

But we feel safe. We feel safer that year, when the Supreme Court makes the call for marriage equality. We drink a toast, though our same sex union was long ago annulled.

We move from that boarding school to another, this one in New Hampshire. I am surprised to learn that the state—alone in New England—doesn't extend civil rights protection to transgender people. Today, a transgender person can be fired for a job because of their identity; can be denied service in a restaurant; can be turned out of housing... And that is perfectly legal.

I go to marches and rallies across the state. I drive to Concord and testify before the state legislature, waiting in a room packed with transgender people, packed with those who believe we don't exist or aren't really human.

We win. It takes two tries, two legislative sessions, and lots of lobbying, but we win. And I go back to the dorm I live in, responsible now for sixty boys, and feel safe. And now, only a few years later, my wife and I sit in my dorm apartment (fireplace, but no flames: fire code says it's a hazard) and read the headlines about the cases going in front of the supreme court. The ones that are trying to strip LGBTQ+ people of their basic civil rights. I try to remember the laughter, the joy, the silliness of having so many rights that I had to get married again.

"LIVES SPLIT ASUNDER"

Jeannine Ouellette

Ten years ago, on December 6th, at age thirty-nine, I stood in an eighth-grade Waldorf classroom in Minneapolis, lighting a beeswax candle. I placed my hands over my heart to say morning verse with the same students I had been teaching for eight years, since they were first graders. They were just months from graduating and leaving the school forever, and I found myself gaping into the jaws of my own future, jaws yawning open and shut, mouthing the brutish question of whether I would ever return to my dream of writing. Sure, I was freelancing for cash—cranking out magazine pieces, contract educational books, ghostwriting projects, the occasional grant—but that's not what my childhood self meant when she proclaimed herself a writer. My childhood self meant novels, even if she didn't know that word or its boundlessness.

As for teaching, it happened accidentally during that summer ten years ago, when my children's school announced a last-minute first grade opening. My then husband and I were accruing debt at the identical rate of tuition payments for our children, who were ten, eight, and five. We couldn't afford Waldorf, but teachers received tuition remission, and the school would overlook my lack of degree—I'd dropped out of college at twenty, with a half-finished English major, to get married and have a baby. We needed two incomes, and the parenting magazine where I'd been editor had recently been swallowed by a conglomerate. Our marriage was bruised enough without more money stress. Plus, I've always loved kids.

So, I leapt.

Into the arms of a new colleague, my son's teacher.

Metaphorical leap, metaphorical arms. But that didn't matter. What mattered is that I pried open the tough fruit of my heart muscle and arranged its bright guilty seeds into a love letter, which my then husband found and shared with our son's teacher's wife, who was also our daughter's teacher. They, too, had three kids at the school.

Lives split asunder.

But this is not about morality or affairs or what qualifies as either. It's not about how, when I married just two years after aging out of foster care—my body a scarecrow of scars from childhood sexual abuse that started when I was four—I was so averse to sex I could barely tolerate my own serrated fingers between my legs. This is not about how that numb girl came back to her senses through a decade of birth, breastfeeding, motherhood, and therapy, or how those visceral experiences wrested her into her pulsing skin and bones just in time to meet a man she would recognize—recognize is the only word for this—as her lover of many lifetimes. This is not even about how that recognition collided with her desperation to be a good mother. In the end, this is about the unlikely grace of scratching through a thicket with no sign of the trail, and the glorious terror of blazing your own.

I loved my children's father, despite profound loneliness. Seeing the bones of our marriage splayed under a mean sun, and walking in the other direction, was harrowing. I shudder just remembering. But I walked anyway, in the only direction I could. I would tell you the suffering wasn't as bad as I feared—but in truth, it was worse. It took a long, long time to recover. I quit the teaching job immediately, but the school said please, we can't lose a first-grade teacher in August, don't add harm to harm. Anyway, being suddenly single, I needed an income more than ever. So, I pressed on, striving to be a good enough mother to make up for splintering my children's family and a good enough teacher to make up for my grand entrance as the school slut. My son's teacher left the school and his own long-estranged marriage. Five years later, we married each other, as my skin and bones sensed we would. The school community, including my students and their parents, made up most of our wedding guests. Over the next decade, our kids began leaping into their lives, too, landing across the globe from Portland, Oregon to Shanghai, China. My children carry my heart in their remarkably soft palms. Meanwhile, my former students—now in their twenties—and their parents remain among my dearest friends. As for my husband—you know the ocean. The ocean carries you. It rocks you while you live and while you die.

And writing. Well, I watched that sweet wax smolder ten years ago, and through the haze, I measured the rows of triangular teeth between me and what I most wanted. I loved teaching and the school—I had toiled to belong there. It was my world. To leave frightened me. But as much as Waldorf teaching ignited my creativity, it also devoured it. To write as I wished, I had to walk in the other direction, again. Once I finally resigned, I landed a university writing position within months, and soon after, I started writing a novel. Then I founded a small creative writing program and committed to finishing my manuscript before I turned fifty. To honor that goal, I applied to an MFA program that, like the Waldorf school, overlooked my lack of degree. Six months ahead of schedule, I'm scrabbling for an agent.

Still, fifty does loom, and time breathes hard through its mouth. Sometimes that terrifies me. But I've been terrified before and kept walking. That, I know, makes all the difference.

"THIS IS WHAT FAITH
DOES"

Sophfronia Scott

It's Monday, December 14th, and I'm back in my home office after dropping my son off on the lush campus of the private school where he's in kindergarten twenty minutes away.

I have goals.

Right now, over one hundred people are registered for a conference call promoting my Business Book Bootcamp in which I teach entrepreneurs how to write books to market their businesses. My goal is to have thirty signups for the program.

I'm ghostwriting two client books with deadline goals.

Today I'm attending two mastermind meetings, support groups with other entrepreneurs, to help me stay on track with these goals.

I'm tired and frustrated. It's been over five years since the publication of my first novel and I've barely made any headway on writing a second, mainly because I've been writing books for other people. Four days earlier I wrote in my journal:

I have decided to do something differently—I am going to apply to an MFA program. The only way I'm going to become the writer I want to be is to put myself in the environment. Something has to change, and this is the right thing to do. It will be a happier goal to shoot for, along the lines of sending Tain to Chase Collegiate. I will begin now.

I'm starving for that happier goal. When my husband and I began discussing private kindergarten where Tain could go full day because our local school, Sandy Hook Elementary, only had half days, the idea had taken flight in my mind with all the quiet, colorful miracle of a hot air balloon. I loved envisioning Tain walking with his friends across the lawn. Now dropping him off each morning feels like an accomplishment. I want to feel a dream like that for myself.

But today I don't know how to begin. Instead of writing novel pages I'm writing marketing emails.

Two years later, after a friend and one of my sisters die within days of each other, I will learn you don't set goals. You just stop. You stop doing what's no longer important. I will stop taking on clients. I will stop hanging out with entrepreneurs. I will enter an MFA program and drive a school bus to help pay for it.

The following year Tain will ask if he can attend school with his godbrothers Nate and Ben and start Sandy Hook Elementary as a third grader. That December I will sit in our church library listening to Tain in the choir across the hall rehearsing Christmas carols. A few days earlier I will have finished the first draft of a novel and begin contemplating the nonfiction one of my new writing friends is encouraging me to write. I will post on Facebook: "Life is good."

I will be glad I wrote those words down. If they had remained pure thought floating through my mind they might have evaporated forever. Because the next morning a gunman named Adam Lanza will blast his way into Tain's school and kill twenty-six adults and children —including Ben. We will live in an ocean of tears. I will fear my heart will sink forever.

But one night I will ask Tain how he's doing and he will say, "Mama, I just have the feeling I'm going to see Ben again. He's going to come down from heaven, and he's going to be here with all of us."

In the days and years to come I will follow Tain's lead and his sense of hope. I will learn from him this is what faith does: it provides buoyancy, allowing you to rise to the surface and not drown in grief.

Ten years from today I will still be driving Tain to school, a commute twice as long, but to a public high school, an arts magnet where he studies theater. I will spend the weekend on retreat at a Kentucky monastery where the Trappist monk and writer Thomas Merton lived. I will pray and work on the book I'm writing about him and my faith journey. I will consider the message I'd written down, "Life is good," grateful for how much I can still believe it.

"CULTIVATING MY OWN
DAMN GARDEN"

Michaella Thornton

Dec
ecember 18th, ten years ago, I pierced my nose for the
first time. I wanted to flash a sign to the outside world
that I was alive and well and still a little wild. I was thirty-one.

There's a selfie of me that day off South Grand. I'm in a
shamrock green peacoat, pierced nose turned to the camera,
smiling with a look of smoldering self-satisfaction. The way
a person looks before loss, before giving birth, before understanding the seismic shift of time unstopped and love unfurled.

In the summer months before that mid-December piercing,
I asked the man I loved to marry me. I was tired of waiting.
We were in Madrid and in love while drinking tiny, cold beers
and eating jamón while watching little girls jump from limb
to limb in an old magnolia tree right outside the Royal Palace.

The first man I ever wanted to marry moved like a glacier, even though I burned like a wildfire, impatient to set
everything ablaze.

But no amount of passion in a sunlit Spanish apartment or
taking a midnight train to Paris or getting lost in the country-
side and stumbling into a bar to ask for directions in broken
French only to sip apple brandy was going to change his pace
or my impatience.

Glaciers operate on geologic time. Wildfires notsomuch.

Maybe if I willed him to love me, I thought, that would be enough.

Turns out one-sided desire doesn't overcome a weak yes. It would take months until I realized my error—after I toured a prospective wedding venue, a Greek Revival mansion built above one of the many caves of St. Louis, and applied for a home loan.

Four months from the next December, we would call off the engagement.

There was a quiet pragmatism in our parting, as if we simply wheeled what little remained out to the curb.

Not many know I was engaged once before.

THE SECOND MAN I WANTED to marry made me laugh and think and played games; far too many games, if you asked me later. At our wedding three years after my engagement to the glacier, the gamer vowed to keep things interesting. But interesting doesn't mean dependable or loving or committed.

"Interesting" is quite often a euphemism for shitty or weird or problematic, isn't it?

A DECADE LATER, I WATCH as the flesh of my seven-year marriage reverts to bone amid twinkling lights as Bing Crosby wishes me days merry and bright.

My divorce will be finalized in a month or so, but I can't help but think of him on bended knee in front of a giant, glittering Christmas tree. I see the fog of his breath and feel my cheeks and fingers go numb as I say yes. We were once in love, truly, on that cold, dark night.

It is also true I no longer burn the way I once did. My hair is gray at the temples. My nose ring is long gone. I care less about flashing signals to the outside world and more about the profound pull of second-act interiority, about cultivating my own damn garden.

I have a young daughter now, whose very existence is wilder than a piece of metal through cartilage. She is everything I have ever looked for in another human being—she grabs my face with both hands when she kisses me, runs into my open arms as she yells "Momma!" and spits bath water at me as I wash her slippery body. She is pure possibility, and I pray every night not to fuck this up.

Ten years ago, no one could have told me that the greatest love of my life would be my child. That the love you have for a partner may dissipate or stall or die, or, for the lucky ones, be remade and reimagined, over and over and over again until growth is what bonds us.

IN 2019, I'LL GO BACK to the photo on South Grand, my fingers tracing the forgotten face of a woman who thought she was so badass rocking a nose ring. She has no clue what the next decade will bring. But who of us does?

"WHAT DOES IT TAKE FOR
A HEART TO STOP?"

Basmah Sakrani

Ten years ago on December 18th, my brother died of a cardiac arrest inside Mirdif City Center, a mall in the desert suburbs of Dubai. He was at an indoor field, warming up for a cricket match with friends, when he collapsed. He was thirty years old. He did not gasp or call out for help. He was gone immediately because his heart had stopped, suddenly. Permanently.

JAWAD SAKRANI WAS BORN on a Friday, an Islamic holy day of congregational prayer and special blessing. I asked my ami about that day; her response was sweet, meandering between memories of her beloved first born. "We were so happy. He was my world, but really it was your Abu who did all the work. He did the bathing and the nighttime feeding and the massaging and the dressing. And it was your uncle who named Jawad. It means generous and noble. I hadn't even thought of a name. He was my special boy, he rubbed my feet and always wanted biryani every Friday."

Bhai, as I called him, was ten years older than me; the main character in photo albums from our childhood in Riyadh, Saudi Arabia. There are pictures of us grinning at our combined birthdays (only eight days apart in June). Black forest cakes with "Sakranis" written in white frosting. Bhai in a prefect's uniform, marching across the auditorium stage to receive his award for Best Quran Recitation. Evenings in the desert, the family barbecuing chicken tikka under the stars. Baby me in a yellow romper on a messy bed, Bhai with his Mr. T mohawk looking at the camera like *She's okay, I guess.*

MY SISTER (BAJI) AND I had been shopping at Mirdif City Center. I was a college sophomore in Lahore, visiting my family in Dubai for winter break and excited to spend the pocket money Bhai had given me that morning. We were in the mall parking lot, about to head home, when Abu called. "Beta, Bhai has collapsed. Come quickly." I mistook my father's even tone for reassurance. *Bhai's being dramatic,* I told myself. *It's not like he's dying.*

The phone rang again. It had only been seconds since the first call.

"Beta, hurry up."

We moved quickly, unbuckling seat belts and slamming doors. Then another, final phone call. "Beta, Bhai has died. Come now." Abu's words were strangled, as though he couldn't quite believe what he was uttering.

It was madness. We sprinted through the mall weeping and screaming. I remember the bright lights of Forever 21, the rush outside Starbucks, and the men in white kanduras, their children shrieking, darting out of our way. I yelled at strangers, pushing and shoving. "Where is the cricket court? I have to get to my brother!" Nothing seemed real until the moment I saw Bhai, his tall, bear-like body, supine on the shiny, vinyl floor. His friends standing in a corner, stricken. A paramedic, packing up. Abu, crying into someone's shoulder.

I remember kneeling, in tears, shaking Bhai, pleading with him to wake up. I argued with the paramedic, a kind Filipino man who teared up and said, "I'm sorry, ma'am, I've tried reviving him six times already." Then I took Bhai's hand, expecting his fingers to grasp mine, but they were cool and unmoving. All I wanted was for him to sit up and say, "Gotcha!" but his eyes were unfocused, devoid of their typical luster. That's when

I realized my brother was dead. I shut his eyelids and kissed his forehead.

WHEN JAWAD WAS EIGHTEEN, he brought home an acoustic guitar and started practicing for hours in the solarium of our Mississauga apartment. He recorded songs, sent them to the Pakistani musicians he idolized. Once, Ali Azmat sent him an email and Bhai went around quoting it to everyone he met. He performed at local desi weddings where he sang Vital Signs covers, some Junoon, always closing with his favorite love song, "Bin Tere Kya Hai Jeena" by his namesake, Jawad Ahmed. He'd come home bubbling about the crowd, the way everyone sang along, and the girls who came up to him after.

Bhai was a true romantic. He fell in love hard and often, skipping school for a picnic date in Niagara Falls, or sleeping through work because he'd spent all night on the phone. Together, Bhai and I kept a tally of his heartbreaks. He grew contemplative and quiet at the end of relationships. Once, he took me to Dairy Queen after a tough breakup. I was ten and he was twenty. We sat in the parking lot, eating our fudgy Peanut Buster Parfaits, Bhai sharing life lessons that I had no way of understanding at the time. "In the end, when the sex and the excitement fades," he said, "you need a friend, a companion. Remember that."

At college he tried out different careers: he worked as a car salesman, then a security guard, and spent almost every Friday at the local mosque in Mississauga. He moved to Dubai when he was twenty-three, became a banker, *and* a romantic to the end, married a girl he fell in love with in only a week. But music remained Bhai's forever love. His wallet held more picks than cash. Old receipts bore fragments of songs in progress. Even after he was married and settled, he went to Karachi to study classical music with an ustad. He returned with a harmonium, another instrument to master. He founded Satwa Sessions, a musical salon in old Dubai where artistes gathered every fortnight to jam. He started a blog, bought a karaoke machine, and threw parties at home, singing to his smiling wife and baby daughter.

WHEN BAJI AND I REACHED home and told Ami that Bhai was dead, she let out a strangled cry and crumpled to the floor. Somehow in her utter wretchedness she managed, in falling, to break a toe. She wore a cast for weeks.

Bhai's funeral took place two days later in Al Quoz cemetery, a sandy graveyard with simple white markers. Following Islamic burial practice, Abu bathed Bhai three times and dressed his body in a plain white shroud, father washing and dressing the son he had cared for as a baby.

When I was finally allowed to see him, Bhai's face was chalky, like it had been salted. His ears and nostrils were stuffed with cotton, and his broad shoulders were cold and blue. Gone was the big brother who once caught his little sister in the kitchen eating Nutella out of a jar with a knife (instead of scolding me, he found me some bread to go with it). Gone was Bhai who used to scare me with made up ghost stories about a spirit called Hawwa Koko, who threatened my boyfriends in high school and got me grounded, who did silly imitations of the delicate Meena Kumari dancing a mujra, his large thumping feet and his XL T-shirt flaring as he twirled. I wept as I said goodbye.

AFTER MY BROTHER'S DEATH, family gatherings were quiet, laced with echoes of his booming voice and heavy footsteps. What does it take for a heart to stop? I kept thinking. I ate nothing for days, trying to see how long I could last on air and grief. I would run for hours, panting and crying, hoping the pain in my legs could overpower my sorrow. What does it take for a heart to stop?

We spoke little of our loss until his daughter Ayana got old enough to demand stories about her baba. In recounting the anecdotes of Bhai's life, and seeing his face in hers, things got better. Not all at once and never entirely. In many ways, Jawad's short life was ordinary. Now, ten years after his death, I can see it was remarkable in how much it contained. The art and music he created, the love he gave out so generously, the places he lived and embodied, the life he created in Ayana. The list is full, even if the years were short. And still, the question remains: what does it take for a heart to stop?

"I'M STILL NOT FRAGILE"

Allison K. Williams

Mexican guidebooks have a lot of rules. Mimi and I have given up on most of them. I'm not-quite divorced, but I'm separated enough to be restless. No one will be stuck looking after me if I get sick; no one has to get a call from the embassy in the middle of the night. Most of the rules sound like they're by and for nervous tourists. I'm a trapeze artist. This is country number thirty-eight. I am not fragile.

Do not eat street food, it may make you sick. Avoid all dairy products as they may not be pasteurized.

But the pushcart vendor pulls roasted ears of corn off a little grill, scrapes the kernels into paper cups with crema, cotija, and lime. The next cart has churros in paper cones. We eat street tacos, sitting on low plastic stools at the Christmas market outside the cathedral.

It is forbidden for foreigners to be part of demonstrations. Avoid large crowds.

Strapped to the roof of my Camry is a bundle of hot-pink poles that build a twenty-two-foot tripod, below which we perform aerial silks and acrobatics and fire-eating in any town where the policemen smile at Mimi's second-year Spanish. She and I have been street-performing together for four years, but this is the first time we're a team of two, the first time we're going wherever we want, no festivals booked, no lodging stipend, no idea where we're allowed to set up. So far, it's going okay. We've eaten fire in Monterrey and Texmelucan, done the whole show in Guanajuato, and learned that in Mexico, street performers pass the hat before the finale. We learned this by collecting the crowd's money and watching them not leave. So we did our regular finale twice.

Do not take pictures of policia, federales, or border guards.

Mexican states have hard borders, with checkpoints and sandbagged sniper nests. Every time, Mexican cars are waved through and we are pulled over. We can't figure it out—they always start half-heartedly searching the car, then stop dead at the box of tampons (now we know where to hide any cocaine).

In Tabasco, we're waved to the side once again, and a cluster of guards with strong Mayan profiles gather around our car. An officer asks my name—not so much "Show me your papers" as "Heyyyy."

The guard rooting in the trunk finds my bullwhips. In the show, I do trick cracking and target-taking, and the popping sounds draw more audience, too. The border guards speak urgently to Mimi, who turns bright red and refuses to translate. She attempts to get the guards on track. Do you want to see our tourist permits? Our passports? They ask if we are married, if they can take a picture, if that one can lift me in his arms.

Never argue with a guy carrying a submachine gun.

The guard comes up to my shoulder, the assault rifle strapped to his back at my eye level. He scoops me into his arms, and his fellow guards line up to snap with their phones. I crack the whip a few times. We pass out bottles of water, repack the trunk and drive off into the jungle, the guards calling after us.

"They want us to meet them at a club in Ciudad del Carmen tonight," Mimi explains. "What he said earlier was, 'Tell her I want her to do bad things to me with the whip.'"

Now we know. We're getting stopped because the border guards are bored. Merry Christmas, guys.

I retired from performing in 2015, and these days, I follow a lot more rules. I use the crosswalk. I don't rush into the middle of crowds that might be a coup. I give officials with guns a wide berth. I'm not afraid for me. I'm still not fragile. But I think of how sad my now-husband would be, spending Christmas without me, how it's not just about my bravery anymore. How caring for him, allowing him to care for me, means sometimes stepping back and watching, keeping safe, taking care of the wife he loves.

"THE FISHING VILLAGE NEAR ZIHUATANEJO"

Debra Gwartney

December 21

Once my husband and I lock the door of the seaside cottage where we've stayed for the past week, we start off on our hour drive. He pulls onto the highway that will take us to the airport outside Zihuatanejo when a truck of armed military police roars up close to our bumper, then swerves to the adjacent lane. I count eight men—four on each bench seat—with automatic weapons strapped across their chests. My glance at them is furtive, over and back. Barry slows to let the truck get well ahead of us. He and I have been in Mexico for a week and this is our first encounter with the country's military presence. We were seven days protected, hidden, from danger or even any hint of violence. And yet here it is now, a reminder of the real world and its hard edges. A reminder that we could barricade ourselves for so long in paradise.

The owner of our cottage—owner of the complex of simple thatched-roof beach homes—bid us goodbye the night before, when she and her husband served us dinner on their patio. I don't remember what we ate except that it was fish and vegetables spiced to perfection. A margarita that sparked in my mouth. Blanca expressed her disappointment that we'd stayed only a brief time. "Next time, two weeks! A month!" she insisted, and

I watched my husband's face wrinkle though he said nothing. I didn't explain that convincing him to come at all was something of a miracle. In our nearly twenty years together, I'd talked him into vacations only twice. Barry traveled extensively—visiting over eighty countries in his lifetime—and I sometimes traveled with him (Greenland, Brazil, Nunavut, Prague)—but he left his home only if he would be fed, nurtured, informed as a writer, or if he could convene with his readers. To go out and, well, basically sit for a string of days made no sense to him.

I'd persuaded my husband to venture out on this second of our two vacations after a friend told us that on this secluded beach there would be no disturbances. Indeed, the weather was mild. Every morning we walked for an hour or two in the golden light of a golden coast and saw no other people, communing only with the coconuts that poked out of the sand like hairy skulls. Our simple cottage was located about a half mile from a fishing village, where electricity was turned off at precisely 8 p.m. As twilight descended, Barry and I strolled down the center of the single residential street, deciding which card table to sit at—one set with utensils and napkins and bottles of unopened beer meant that the woman (at least we saw only women) of the house was prepared to cook dinner for a stranger. Plates loaded with fish and rice and beans, and more of the spicy, pungent squash and peppers. We ate our fill and then some. We drank warm beer from bottles. We left pesos on the vinyl surface of the table, and walked home in the dark, lured and guided by the sound of ocean waves.

As days passed, I witnessed a kind of melting in Barry. His shoulders let go. He wore flip-flops and shorts. He tipped back in a chair and sipped coffee, staring out at the sea, reading book after book, saying little. We rented kayaks and made our way through thick brush to the mangrove swamps, populated with so many birds their songs made it hard for us to hear each other. Osprey fished alongside our boats and we called to them, certain that these were the osprey of our own river, the McKenzie in western Oregon, and that we would greet them again come

April, when we'd awaken one morning to their crisp chirps in our clear blue sky.

What did we talk about during our hours in Mexico? I hardly remember. We had no television, no internet service. I can't recall a source of music. We found peace in a kind of silence that we, as a couple, had not experienced before. What we didn't bring up was Barry's diagnosis. I'd been with him in the urologist's office a few months before this trip to take in the news of prostate cancer, stage 4, already in his bones and in his lymph nodes. There was no possibility of cure, only a barrage of treatments meant to prevent the invasion from progressing, though of course it would progress. The cancer would, inevitably, beat out attempts to hold it back. But good news, the oncologist said: it could take years.

What could we expect during those promised years? How were we to prepare? These were questions I asked myself as I wandered into the warm water one day, knees wobbling against the pull of the tide. I thought that during our stay here, we'd parse a plan, design an approach to whatever was ahead for us. Though of course what folly to believe that was possible. I had no idea of the plethora of drugs Barry would endure. I couldn't yet fathom the myriad health complications that would arise once his body was assailed by the poisons meant to keep him alive. The diets we'd try, the books and articles we'd read, the unbidden advice from every corner. Nor could I predict yet my exhaustion and frustration—arguments that wounded and polarized us until, spent, we somehow managed to find our way to each other again.

All of that was in the future. The only thing to do now was to get back on my feet after being flattened by a wave and scramble to shore, waving at my husband who was staying cool on the porch, sliding a sliver of orange papaya into his mouth as if it was a goldfish wriggling in his belly, licking his sticky fingers and reaching for another.

EXACTLY SEVEN YEARS AFTER we departed from this secluded corner of Mexico—a village whose name I can't recall though

I would have said back then that I could never forget—our family came to say goodbye to Barry. December 21, 2020. Four daughters—his step-daughters—with their spouses and children. He stayed in bed most of the day now, but he got up for a few hours and we nestled him into a comfortable chair in the living room. The children hugged him and kissed him and laughed with him, and when he grew too weak to keep on, they put on their hats and coats and disappeared into the bitter cold. The next morning the daughters would return by themselves, and we would hold vigil until the moment of his death at 7:20 p.m. on Christmas Day.

For some years—2014 and 2015, maybe even longer—Barry and I talked about returning to the fishing village near Zihuatanejo, promising ourselves another stretch of peace and calm. But it never happened, and then he was too sick to travel. On Christmas Eve of 2020, I climbed into bed with him, a narrow hospital bed so that I had to teeter and cling to the edge. Barry was in a morphine haze, his mouth open to suck in air, his face ashen and smooth. Lying next to him, I remembered an afternoon in Mexico when he'd rolled into the outdoor hammock. The post that held one end of the hammock creak-creaked with the subtle movement of his body. I was reading in a chair nearby and he reached out to take my hand. He squeezed it hard as if to say, *Don't worry. We'll find our way through this. We'll figure it out together. It's all going to be okay.*

"AMERICAN HUSTLE"

Grant Faulkner

December 29

Opening scene: I'm working on my laptop on my parents' couch in their home in Oskaloosa, Iowa. I've flown there from San Francisco. I have a migraine. One of my first migraines ever, so I don't even know that it's a migraine. I only know my head hurts worse than a normal headache, and the words stumble awkwardly from my brain to the page and back.

I'm putting the finishing touches on a year-end fundraising appeal for the creative writing nonprofit I lead. Here's the thing about being the executive director of a nonprofit: you always need money. You can never rest. Even on your birthday. Yes, it's my birthday, my forty-ninth birthday, and I'm a birthday person, a self-indulgent and just plain selfish birthday person, and I'm chagrined that the world doesn't support good causes enough to give me a break on my birthday.

But I don't write that. I write how stories connect us, how our imagination transforms the world in magical ways, how the world progresses one story at a time. I believe all of that deeply, I've devoted my life to it, but I have a migraine, and the noise of my family in the kitchen is making it difficult to write. Not just the noise, but their togetherness. Which I want to be a part of.

Birthdays are a time for math. There are the eras when getting older is a good thing—when you're sixteen and can drive a car, when you become an official adult at eighteen, when you turn nineteen and can drink (at least in my era); each year promising new adventures, new opportunities. But then there are the eras where you get older—older as in older, as in leaving things behind—and while you might say age holds new adventures, one of those adventures is the end of age: death. And it's getting closer. When I turned forty, I remarked to a friend who was in his seventies that forty was the new thirty. He told me, no, forty is forty.

So I must have been thinking something like, *Oh, shit, forty-nine years old, that means I'm going to be fifty next year, which means I'm old, officially old.* It's true, the AARP sends you its initial barrage of never-ending mail when you turn fifty. But since I was still just forty-nine, a young'un, I didn't yet know how different my fifties would be: how mortality peeks its head over the horizon and winks at you, and then, now that I'm fifty-nine, how I see it staring at me with a menacing glare.

I'm a selfish birthday person for several reasons. One, because I'm a middle child, so I'm hard wired to lay claim to any moment where I can get attention. To add to my chip on my shoulder, my birthday falls on a day right in the cross-hairs between Christmas and New Year's, when no one really wants to celebrate it. Several years before this, after a string of neglected and dispiriting birthdays, I was on a vacation with friends. When I asked them to join me for a few birthday drinks in the hot tub, I could tell they were too pooped to celebrate. Even on a vacation. I resigned myself to sitting in the jacuzzi alone with a cold beer until one self-sacrificing friend joined me, clearly out of duty.

I made the promise then that I'd celebrate all future birthdays by myself. It would be a day without the complications of others. I would decide exactly what I wanted to do and experience it alone. This worked because I love being alone, and, especially after years of parenthood, solitude is its own magical gift. So, a tradition was born, and I loved my solitary birthdays—birthdays of espresso and Italian pastries at Café Trieste in North Beach, a day at the Kabuki Hot Springs, martinis accompanied by a jukebox full of Maria Callas' opera at Strada—all in the same day!

But on this day, December 29, 2013, I had to sacrifice my streak of fulsome, decadent birthdays to come home with my brother and sister to visit my parents because they'd suddenly become too old to travel to see us for the holidays.

Once I finished my fundraising appeal, I made my way to the kitchen, and everyone asked me what I wanted to do for my birthday. The pickings were slim. The choices were a movie, or a movie. Fortunately, *American Hustle* was playing at a tawdry cineplex on the outskirts of Ottumwa. With a population of 25,000, twice that of Oskaloosa, it had a Target, whereas we only had a Kmart. That might not mean much to someone not from the Midwest, but it was all you needed to know about the difference between the two towns. Oskaloosa was decidedly a blue-light special kind of town.

I'd always had a fascination with Ottumwa. My father told me it was once known as "Little Chicago" because of its mafia connections. It was a river town. A meat packing town. A rough place. Its claim to fame was that it was the birthplace of Radar O'Reilly from *M*A*S*H*, and then later, notoriously, to Tom Arnold (Roseanne Barr's ex-husband). Perhaps its most significant citizen, though, was Tom Arnold's sister Lori, known as the "Queen of Meth," because she had a meth production and distribution operation based on a 170-acre ranch outside Ottumwa that grossed more than $200,000 per week at its peak. It turns out some Iowans had a taste for meth.

But that's a story for another time.

We drove to Ottumwa, the five of us in a single car. It was one of those cold, windswept Iowa winter days. The kind where all of the leaves have been stripped from the trees and the frozen hardness of the ground permeates the feel of life. It was a day of grayness, a hard, gun-metal grayness. A relentless grayness. A grayness that put in question why anyone stayed in this place, why my family had farmed on this land for generations in a losing battle to make a living. I loved this land so much, though. Perhaps because its bareness had, in its strange way, invited my dreams to exist.

The cineplex usually just showed superhero and action movies, so the fact that *American Hustle* was showing was a small miracle. It was a film made by one of my favorite directors, David O. Russell, and starred Christian Bale, Amy Adams, Jennifer Lawrence, and Bradley Cooper. It was a movie about people doing con jobs in order to be real in life—to touch something bigger through power and money. Gaudy seventies garb. Characters on the brink of imploding. Everyone wanting. And wanting more. Christian Bale had a belly the size of a beer keg and a torturously complicated comb-over that made me pledge to start taking better care of myself. Even though everyone was scamming each other, somehow a genuine love survived at the center of it all. It was a movie about the reinvention of self. A theme for every birthday.

Afterward, we drove around Ottumwa's deserted streets looking for a restaurant to eat in. I was hopeful we could find a classic Iowa steakhouse, but there was nothing open that looked appetizing. The curse of my birthday had returned. We decided to drive home and eat leftovers.

As we drove, we were cloaked in a drape of quiet darkness, skitters of snow shooting into the headlights. We'd been together so often on such drives, driving home from Des Moines after a day of shopping, a performance at the Civic Center, a day at the art museum. We could be defined as a family in motion, moving away from our small town toward any sophistication we could cull from our nearby surroundings, eventually moving away to a bigger world beyond Iowa. We were fundamentally creatures of aspiration. My father was the first from his family to leave the farm and go to college, and then he became a lawyer who was known as the best-dressed man in town. My mother, an antique collector, made our home into a decorator's showcase. My brother moved to Los Angeles to work with celebrities to decorate their homes. My sister left to go to an Ivy League school. And I set out to write stories about other places, and to live a life worthy of stories.

That was the last time we were in a car together, just the five of us. My parents' health quickly declined afterward. My father would be dead in just four years.

Now, ironically, I take the same heart medications that he took in his final years. All of life has been similar to writing that fundraising appeal: having a vision, trying to transform life into something better, asking the world for support, working to the point of exhaustion. I drank too much. I slept too little. I asked too much of life. I asked too much of myself. As Christian Bale learned in the movie, there are only so many ways to try to comb your hair over to cover your baldness.

Birthdays are about math. With my heart condition, my odds of being alive five years from now are supposedly only fifty percent. Who knows. I eat my broccoli. I don't drink my drinks. I pray to a God I don't believe in. But math, as much as it might damn, also gives clarity. When I think back to this day now, this day I wanted more from, I wouldn't trade it for any of the pleasures I would have soaked myself in if I'd celebrated the day by myself in San Francisco.

A good birthday is simply one that happens, I now know. Preferably with others.

EPILOGUE

I can lose myself in a moment, my mind drifting away from present tense, toward a memory that's nearly tangible. Yesterday, I time-traveled twenty-five years ago and climbed sand dunes nestled along northern Lake Michigan while my mother watched the waves roll in, closer to shore. The flashback smells like her go-to lake staples: smoked whitefish, Made Rite White Cheddar popcorn, and Faygo Rock & Rye. Every time I water my plants, I pass by my dog's ashes and find myself back to January 3rd, 2021, saying goodbye to him for the last time. These moments cause me to shiver, maybe because the day he left, the ground was saturated in cold and white. Maybe because any time I think about death, I'm overwhelmed with both heartache and some kind of temporal claustrophobia that makes the world feel a bit chillier.

When I come back to the present, I've lost time—a few seconds, maybe a thousand years. I'm so overcome with the act of remembering, the present is disrupted. This is why my partner, Donald Quist, sometimes worries how I can lean too easily into nostalgia. This concern reinforces how we often are foils to one another: he's worried I have some kind of undeniable kink for nostalgia, and I worry his obsession with the present is another way to avoid the joy and pain of remembering.

Nostalgia always gets a bad rap, though it really doesn't have a choice in late-stage capitalism, where virtue is placed on productivity and what comes next. In this climate, slowing down is a character flaw. We don't have room for things we've moved on from the week before, much less a more distant past.

Our brains are weighed down by amassing checklists, never-ending digital notifications, and a looming dread regarding the increasing cost of living.

Author Michael Chabon's definition of nostalgia is more digestible:

> The feeling that overcomes you when some minor vanished beauty of the world is momentarily restored, whether summoned by art or by the accidental enchantment of a painted advertisement for Sen-Sen, say, or Bromo-Seltzer, hidden for decades, then suddenly revealed on a brick wall when a neighboring building is torn down. In that moment, you are connected; you have placed a phone call directly into the past and heard an answering voice.

On an atomic level, Chabon looks at nostalgia as "the ache that arises from the consciousness of lost connection." The German language uses the word, *sehnsucht*, to describe an ineffable kind of yearning or craving that comes with nostalgia, or even when thinking about the present and future. *Sehnsucht* can stem from something unknown or unfinished, but it's not necessarily good or bad. It's a deep emotional experience that, while all-encompassing, is just momentary.

I think this perception of nostalgia is more in line with Donald's philosophy. His biggest worry stems from him knowing my brain and how I process things, how I can feel too much. He's cognizant of my capacity to get lost in a moment as well as my anxiety regarding time, which gives me a feeling of *sehnsucht* when I think about it for too long. It's also more in line with his philosophy because he created *Past Ten*, a project that forces you to reach back in time in order to strengthen our understanding of the present.

In these moments of remembrance, we're offered an opportunity to reconnect to something lost in the corners of our memory and to make sense of it. Perhaps losing yourself in a moment—losing time—is necessary for a healthy relationship with the present. This is why *Past Ten* resonates with our contributors and, in turn, our readers. It's a project rooted in time and nostalgia and being, which fundamentally calls its writers to reflect on the relationship between former and current selves.

I hope reading this anthology allowed you to slow down with each reflection, notice the different ways each author restored something previously vanished from their world from ten years ago. Like Kali White VanBaale wrote in the introduction, there is a magic to *Past Ten*. It comes in the form of a randomly assigned date resonating with a writer. Maybe the prompt itself has some magic because it encourages the writer to be more vulnerable. The biggest magic we could ever hope for is the quietest—a shift in energy and perspective, where emptiness feels a little lighter knowing this *now* will someday be a *then*. That there can be hope and change—that you can create your own timeline. In this sense, maybe my chronophobia has betrayed me, and the real magic this whole time was time, itself.

—Bailey Gaylin Moore
Editor-In-Chief of *Past Ten*

Where were you on this day ten years ago?

Dear Reader,

We at *The Past Ten* know every person has a journey and story, and that sharing these stories can be profoundly useful in understanding who we are today.

We want you to ponder yours in 1000 words or less.

Start with today's date: _____

Then think about the question: *where were you on this day ten years ago?*

Where were you living? Where were you working? What did your life look like at that time? What successes were you experiencing, or what struggles were you working through at that time? Consider what your life looks like today. How is it different, how has it changed? How are *you* different or changed? What has been your journey these past ten years?

Now, tell your story.

Feel like sharing your story? We'd love to read it.

Visit us at past-ten.com.

CONTRIBUTORS

Diannely Antigua is a Dominican American poet and educator, born and raised in Massachusetts. She is the author of the Whiting Award-winning collection *Ugly Music* (2019) and *Good Monster* (2024). She received her MFA at NYU and hosts the podcast *Bread & Poetry*.

Refael Paul Arenson's words appear in *North American Review*, *The Bombay Literary Magazine* and other venues, and are online at Utne Reader and Art Daily. He tinkers with fiction, nonfiction and poetry, and also translates from French and Italian. Arenson's an MFA graduate from Vermont College of Fine Arts. Instagram and TwitterX: @refaelpaulo.

Elizabeth Austin's writing has appeared on *Tor.com*, *PANK*, *Driftwood Press*, and *Sybil*, among others. She holds an MFA from Vermont College of Fine Arts. Her works-in-progress include a memoir about her daughter's three years of leukemia treatment and a novel about a ghost. She lives in Bucks County with her two children, their Newfoundland Numa, their black cat Zoro, and a hamster named Wednesday. Instagram: @writingelizabeth.

Nikki Boss publishes both creatively and academically. She's the author of the chapbook *Bar Yarns for the Average American* and under "Nikki Anderson" publishes scholarship, most recently a co-edited collection *Class, Identity and Finding the Right Wine in Schitt's Creek* (2024). Nikki is the founder of the indie lit journal *Skink Beat Review* and currently serves as assistant professor of English at Nichols College in Dudley, MA.

Renee Brown lives in Springfield, Misouri, with her husband, Jason, and two dogs who are much more photogenic than their humans. She is a technical writer for a software company, and enjoys baking grumpy snowmen cookies, too many types of crafts, and watching the YouTubes.

Aaron Burch is the author of the essay collection *A Kind of In-Between* and the novel, *Year of the Buffalo*. He is the editor of *HAD* and *Short Story, Long*.

Natalie Byers is a parent, writer, and teacher from Columbia, Missouri. They hold master's degree from MSU and Vermont College of Fine Arts. Their work can be found in *Foothill*, *Witness*, *Fugue*, and *Slipstream*. Collections include *The Great and Terrible* and *The Farmer's Wives in Three Acts* (2021).

Mathieu Cailler is the author of seven books. His stories, poems, and essays have appeared in over one hundred publications, including the *Saturday Evening Post* and the *Los Angeles Times*. Feel free to connect with him on social media @writesfromla or at mathieucailler.com.

Caylin Capra-Thomas's poetry collection, *Iguana Iguana*, was named a Best New Poetry Book for Adults by the New York Public Library. Her recent work has appeared in *The Georgia Review* and *cream city review*. A recipient of fellowships from Vermont Studio Center, Sewanee Writers Conference, and the Studios of Key West, she was the 2018-2020 poet-in-residence at Idyllwild Arts Academy and is currently a PhD candidate in English and creative writing at the University of Missouri.

Ann Dávila Cardinal is the author of the YA horror novel *Five Midnights* and received the 2020 International Latino Book Award in the Best Young Adult Fantasy & Adventure category and was finalist for the Bram Stoker Award, as well as the YA novels *Category Five* and *Breakup From Hell*, and adult novels *The Storyteller's Death* and *We Need No Wings*. Her stories have appeared in *Other Terrors: An Inclusive Anthology*, *Lockdown: Stories of Crime, Terror, and Hope During a Pandemic*, and *Our Shadows Have Claws*.

Kathryn Caves is a comedy writer based in New York City. Her work has appeared on the humor websites *Weekly Humorist*, *The Daily Drunk*, and *Little Old Lady Comedy*. Kathryn is a Doctor of Pharmacy, but please don't ask her to identify any loose pills.

Tyrese L. Coleman is a writer, wife, mother, and attorney. Her debut collection of stories and essays, *How to Sit*, was published in 2018 and nominated for a 2019 PEN Open Book Award. Her work has appeared as a notable in Best American Essays 2018 and 2016 and nominated for a Pushcart Prize.

Ryan Collins is the author of *A New American Field Guide & Song Book*, and several chapbooks. He is the Executive Director of the Midwest Writing Center, and hosts the SPECTRA Reading Series in Rock Island, IL, where he lives.

Joel Coltharp lives in Springfield, Missouri, where he is a Senior Instructor of creative writing and literature at Missouri State University. He also serves as Fiction Editor for *Moon City Review*.

Brandon Daily is the author of the novels *A Murder Country*, *The Valley*, and *Through the Dark* as well as *Darkening*, a collection of fiction. He is a graduate of Lindenwood University's MFA program and lives in New England with his wife and two children.

Jacqueline Doyle's creative nonfiction has appeared in *EPOCH*, *Fourth Genre*, and *The Gettysburg Review*, and has been awarded nine Notable Essay citations in Best American Essays. Her flash fiction chapbook *The Missing Girl* is available from Black Lawrence Press. She lives in Castro Valley, in the San Francisco Bay Area. Find her online at jacquelinedoyle.com and on X @ doylejacq.

Grant Faulkner is the co-founder of *100 Word Story*, the co-host of the *Write-minded* podcast, and the former Executive Director of National Novel Writing Month (NaNoWriMo). He recently published *The Art of Brevity: Crafting the Very Short Story*. He's published several collections of short stories, and his stories have appeared in dozens of literary magazines and been anthologized widely. Find him at grantfaulkner.com

Kathy Fish's stories have been published in *Ploughshares*, *Denver Quarterly*, *Electric Literature*, *Best American Nonrequired Reading*, the *Norton Reader*, and *Norton's Flash Fiction America*. Her honors include the Copper Nickel Editor's Prize and a Ragdale Foundation Fellowship. She publishes a popular monthly craft newsletter, *The Art of Flash Fiction*.

Stephen Furlong is a writer currently residing in Saint Louis, Missouri. His work can be found in *Delta Poetry Review*, *Jarfly*, and *Pine Hills Review*, among others. His chapbook, *What Loss Taught Me*, was published in 2018. He currently serves as a Chapbook Editor for the Garden Party Collective.

Amanda Futrell lives in Seattle and works in consumer journalism as an editor and project manager. She plays pinball poorly and is currently overwhelmed by her sixty-eight plants. Her fiction can be found in *Minerva Rising*, *See Spot Run*, and elsewhere.

Gra[c]e "Grae" Gardiner is a British-American non-binary poet, scholar, public library worker, burgeoning intermedia installation artist, and goose. Find them online at pearlsthatwere.tumblr.com.

Scott Garson is the author of the story collection *Is That You, John Wayne?* and is the editor of *Wigleaf*. He lives in central Missouri.

Wandeka Gayle is a Jamaican-born writer, visual artist, and Assistant Professor of Creative Writing at Spelman College. She's the author of *Motherland and Other Stories* and received the 2023 Solstice Fiction Prize, and numerous writing fellowships. She's a 2023 UNCF/Mellon Fellow and holds a PhD in English. Other writing has appeared in *Prairie Schooner*, *The Rumpus*, *Transition*, and *Interviewing the Caribbean*.

June Gervais's novel *Jobs for Girls with Artistic Flair* (Viking/Penguin) is the coming-of-age story of a young queer woman apprenticing as a tattoo artist in the mostly male industry of the 1980s. Her work appears in *Lit Hub*, *Writer's Digest*, *Sojourners*, *Big Fiction*, *North American Review*, and elsewhere. Find her at junegervais.com.

Samuel Gilpin is a poet living in Portland, Oregon, who holds a PhD in English literature from the University of Nevada, Las Vegas, which explains why he works as a door-to-door salesman. He has served as the Poetry Editor of *Witness Magazine* and Book Review Editor of *Interim*, with his work appearing in various journals and magazines, most recently in *The Bombay Gin*, *Omniverse*, and *Colorado Review*.

Anne Gimm writes fiction and personal essays. A former lawyer, she earned her MFA from Vermont College of Fine Arts and her BA in English from Yale, and her work has been supported by VONA and the One Story Writers' Conference. She is a daughter of Korean War survivors and lives with her family in Montclair, New Jersey.

Christopher Gonzalez is the author of *I'm Not Hungry but I Could Eat: Stories* (2021). A 2021 NYFA/NYSCA Artist Fellow in Fiction and co-fiction editor for *Barrelhouse* magazine, he splits his time between Brooklyn, New York, and Providence, Rhode Island, and lives on various social media platforms @ livesinpages.

Kelle Groom is the author of *How to Live: A Memoir in Essays* and *I Wore the Ocean in the Shape of a Girl*—a B&N Discover Great New Writers selection and *New York Times Book Review* Editor's Choice—and four poetry collections, most recently *Spill*. A National Endowment for the Arts Fellow, Mass Cultural Council Fellow, and two-time Florida Book Award winner, Groom's work appears in *American Poetry Review*, *Best American Poetry*, *The New Yorker*, *New York Times*, *Ploughshares*, and *Poetry*. She's a Nonfiction Editor at *AGNI Magazine*.

Heather Gudenkauf is the Edgar Award nominated, *New York Times*, and *USA Today* bestselling author of ten novels, including *The Weight of Silence*, *The Overnight Guest*, and *Everyone Is Watching*. She lives in Iowa with her family. "I'm Struck By How Upbeat I Sound" by Heather Gudenkauf. Copyright © 2019 by Heather Gudenkauf. All rights reserved. By arrangement with the author.

Debra Gwartney's memoir, *Live Through This*, was a National Book Critics Circle Award finalist, and *I Am a Stranger Here Myself*, won the RiverTeeth Nonfiction Prize and Willa Award for Nonfiction. She's published in *Granta*, *The Sun*, *Tin House*, *American Scholar*, *The Normal School*, *Creative Nonfiction*, *Modern Love*, and others. She's received two Pushcart Prizes and selected for *Best American Essays*, is a contributing editor for *Poets & Writers*, and co-edited *Home Ground: Language for an American Landscape* with late husband Barry Lopez. She lives in Oregon.

Amanda Hadlock is an MFA candidate in Creative Writing at Florida State University, where she's Assistant Editor for the *Southeast Review*, and received her MA in English from Missouri State University. Her nonfiction, fiction, and graphic narrative work has appeared in *Cleaver Magazine*, NPR/WFSU's All Things Considered, *Essay Daily*, *Fractured Literary's* second anthology volume, *Hobart After Dark*, *Wigleaf*, *New Limestone Review*, *The Florida Review*, and others.

Veronica Daehn Harvey earned her MFA in Writing from Lindenwood University in 2020 and her Bachelor of Journalism from the University of Nebraska-Lincoln in 2002. A Nebraska native, she now lives in Colorado with her husband and three children. A former newspaper reporter, she now teaches high school English.

Jon Hickey is a writer in San Francisco. His stories have appeared in the *Virginia Quarterly Review*, *Gulf Coast*, and the *Massachusetts Review*. His debut novel, *Big Chief*, was published in 2025.

Pete Hsu is the author of the short story collection *If I Were The Ocean, I'd Carry You Home* and the experimental chapbook *There Is A Man*. His writing has been featured in *The Los Angeles Review*, *The Bare Life Review*, *F(r)iction Magazine*, *Faultline*, and others. He was a 2017 PEN America Emerging Voices Fellow and the 2017 PEN in the Community Writer in Residence. He was born in Taipei, Taiwan and currently resides in Southern California.

Cherryl Jensen lives in Easthampton, Massachusetts. She received her MFA from Vermont College of Fine Arts in 2022. Her writing has appeared in *Persimmon Tree*, *Concrete Wolf*, *Northern New England Review*, *Psychiatric Services*, and more.

Anu Kumar lives in New Jersey and holds an MFA in writing from Vermont College of Fine Arts. Her work has appeared in *The Missouri Review*, *The Common*, *On The Seawall*, *Catamaran Literary Reader*, *The Maine Review*, *Litro Magazine*, *Scroll.in* and elsewhere. She's the author of the collection *A Sense of Time and Other Stories* and the novel *The Kidnapping of Mark Twain: A Bombay Mystery*. She received a notable mention in the 2023 *Best American Essays*.

Caitlin Kunkel's work has been featured in *The New Yorker*, *McSweeney's*, on public radio, and more. She co-founded the comedy site The Belladonna and the Satire and Humor Festival, created the online satire writing program for The Second City, and teaches workshops across the U.S. and internationally. Her first book, *New Erotica for Feminists*, was named 1 of the Ten Best Comedy Books of the Year by *Vulture*. Her second book, *Inside Jokes: A Comedy and Creativity Guide For All Writers*, is forthcoming in 2026.

Amy Lee Lillard is the author of *Exile in Guyville*, winner of the 2022 BOA Editions Short Fiction Prize, *A Grotesque Animal*, and *Dig Me Out*. She is the co-creator of Broads and Books Productions, creating podcasts, publications, and presses. Find her at amyleelillard.com.

Patrick Madden is the author of three essay collections: *Disparates* (2020), *Sublime Physick* (2016), and *Quotidiana* (2010). He is co-editor of the journal *Fourth Genre* and the 21st Century Essays series at Ohio State University Press, as well as vice president of the NonfictioNOW conference. He teaches at Brigham Young University and Vermont College of Fine Arts.

Kim Magowan is the author of the short story collection *How Far I've Come* (2022), the novel *The Light Source* (2019), and the short story collection *Undoing* (2018). Her stories have been selected for Best Small Fictions and *Wigleaf's* Top 50. She is the Editor-in-Chief and Fiction Editor of *Pithead Chapel*.

Cassidy McCants received her MFA in fiction from Vermont College of Fine Arts. She's the creator/editor of *Apple in the Dark*. Her prose has appeared in *Grist, Clackamas Literary Review, The Plentitudes*, and elsewhere, and she won the 2020 Innovative Short Fiction Contest from *The Conium Review*.

Miriam McEwen writes about disability and bodily autonomy. Her work is anthologized in *Best Small Fictions* and appears in *Black Warrior Review*, *SAND Journal*, *HAD*, and elsewhere. An associate editor at the *South Carolina Review*, Miriam holds an MFA in Writing from Vermont College of Fine Arts. She lives in the foothills of South Carolina. Find her on Instagram @miriammcewen.

Jeni McFarland holds an MFA from the University of Houston where she served as fiction editor for *Gulf Coast* magazine. She is a Kimbilio Fellow, with an essay appearing in *The Beiging of America* (2Leaf Press, 2017). She lives in rural Michigan with her husband. *The House of Deep Water* (Putnam, 2020) was her first novel.

Jasminum McMullen's last three streams were *Baddies*, *Bob's Burgers*, and *Back to Black*. Her writing has appeared in *A Gathering Together*, *midnight & indigo*, *Baby Teeth*, *The Elevation Review*, and anthologized in *Black Joy Unbound* (2023) and *Mamas, Martyrs, and Jezebels* (2024).

Chital Mehta is the winner of the 2022 *SLAB* magazine contest and a finalist for 2022 The Pinch Literary Contest. She is working on her novel *Have You Seen Sumit?* in which a middle-aged woman sets out on a harrowing journey to find her missing son.

Damien Miles-Paulson lives in Portland, OR, where he rides his bike and teaches High School.

Alex Myers is a teacher, speaker, and advocate for transgender rights. His novels include *Revolutionary* (2014) and *The Story of Silence* (2020). His nonfiction book, *Supporting Transgender Students,* will have a second edition in 2024. He is the Director of the Mountain School of Milton Academy.

Phong Nguyen is the author of two story collections and three novels, including *Bronze Drum* and *Roundabout*. He is a professor at the University of Missouri, where he teaches fiction writing.

Michael Nye is the author of three books of fiction, most recently the story collection *Until We Have Faces*. His writing has appeared in *Epoch*, *Boulevard*, *Kenyon Review*, *North American Review*, *The Millions*, and elsewhere. He lives with his family in Ohio, and works as the editor of *Story*.

Liza Olson is the author of the novels *Here's Waldo*, *The Brother We Share*, and *Afterglow*. A Best of the Net nominee, Best Small Fictions nominee, finalist for *Glimmer Train's* Very Short Fiction Award, and 2021 *Wigleaf* longlister in and from Chicagoland, she's been published in *SmokeLong Quarterly*, *Cleaver*, *Pithead Chapel*, and others. One of her proudest achievements was running *(mac)ro(mic)* for four incredible years. lizaolsonbooks.com @lizaolsonbooks.

Jeannine Ouellette's *The Part That Burns* was a *Kirkus* Best 100 and finalist for the Next Generation Indie Book Award. Her writing appears widely and she teaches at the University of Minnesota, the Minnesota Prison Writing Workshop, and Writing in the Dark, a thriving creative community she founded in 2020.

Gwendolyn Paradice is queer, hard of hearing, and a citizen of the Cherokee Nation. Their first book, the short story collection *More Enduring For Having Been Broken*, was the 2019 Hudson winner from Black Lawrence Press. Their fiction and nonfiction have been published in *Booth*, *Crab Orchard Review*, *The Journal of American Folklore*, and *Tin House Online* among others.

Kevin Prufer's newest books are *The Fears* and *Sleepaway: a Novel.* Among his eight others are *Churches*, named one of the best ten books of 2015 by *The New York Times*, and *How He Loved Them*, long-listed for the 2019 Pulitzer Prize and recipient of the Julie Suk Award for the best poetry book from an American literary press. Prufer's work appears widely in *Best American Poetry*, The Pushcart Prize Anthology, *The Paris Review*, and *The New Republic*, among others.

Jennifer Pun is a film & television producer. Her credits include award-winning series *How To Be Indie*, features Fall, *The Void* and *Netflix Top Ten Cascade* among others. Jennifer holds an MFA in Writing from Vermont College of Fine Arts. An instructor at San Diego Writers Ink, her latest work can be found in the anthology *Modern Metamorphoses: Stories of Transformation.*

Katie Quach is a former teacher and writer currently living in Ho Chi Minh City, Vietnam. She was born in Northfield, Minnesota. She's lived in Flatbush, Lopburi, Hanoi, Mexico City, Alameda, and San Francisco, but considers California her home. She is an alumna of the Tin House Writers Workshop and Vermont College of Fine Arts MFA in Creative Nonfiction. She is slowly, slowly working on her first book.

Rima Rantisi is a lecturer at the American University of Beirut and the founding editor of *Rusted Radishes: Beirut Literary and Art Journal.* Her essays can be found in the *New England Review*, *Literary Hub*, and other places. She holds an MFA from Vermont College of Fine Arts and has received literary fellowships from Headlands Center for the Arts and Hedgebrook.

Sage Ravenwood is a deaf Cherokee woman residing in upstate New York. Her work can be found in *The Temz Review*, *Contrary*, *Grain*, *The Rumpus*, and *Lit Quarterly*. *Everything That Hurt Us Becomes a Ghost* is her exploration of the lingering trauma of familial violence and the machinations of colonialism.

Lacey Rowland is an artist and writer from the west. Their work has appeared in *Moss, Tahoma Literary Review, Hobart, Cutbank, Pleiades,* and elsewhere. They received their MFA in Creative Writing from Oregon State University.

JJ Rushing's longest held love has been poetry. She has studied with wonderful artists, most prominently Diane di Prima, for whom she is eternally grateful. JJ has worked as an editor, teacher, and freelance writer. She is most proud of her original curriculum in her writing workshop series, "The Writer's Road."

Basmah Sakrani is a 2024 Veasna So Scholar in Fiction and finalist for the Kinder/Crump Short Fiction Award. She writes about diaspora and loss and is featured in *CRAFT, The Adroit Journal* and more. Basmah works in advertising in New York City. Follow her on Substack: basmah.substack.com.

Adam Sawyer is an outdoor and travel writer, photographer, published author, guide, and public speaker based in the Northwest. In addition to authoring numerous guidebooks, his work has appeared in several local and national outlets. His weekly Substack newsletter, *Collecting Sunsets,* covers a broad set of topics including grief, addiction and recovery, travel, and the healing powers of nature.

Rion Amilcar Scott is the author of the story collections *The World Doesn't Require You* and *Insurrections,* which was awarded the 2017 PEN/Bingham Prize for Debut Fiction and the 2017 Hillsdale Award from the Fellowship of Southern Writers. He teaches creative writing at the University of Maryland. His work has appeared in *The New Yorker, The Kenyon Review, Best American Science Fiction and Fantasy 2020,* and *McSweeney's Quarterly,* among others.

Sophfronia Scott is a leading contemplative thinker who writes nonfiction books, including *The Seeker and the Monk, Love's Long Line,* and *This Child of Faith,* and novels, including *Wild,*

Beautiful, and Free, Unforgivable Love, and *All I Need to Get By*. She is founding director of Alma College's MFA in Creative Writing, a graduate program located in Alma, Michigan.

Gaurra Shekhar was the co-editor in chief of *No Contact*, and the author of *Notes*. In memoriam: 1995–2022.

James Bernard Short's (Bernard James) work has appeared in *Auburn Avenue, Callaloo*, and *Blood Orange Review*, among other journals and literary publications. In addition to being awarded fellowships from Kimbilio and the Givens Foundation for AFAM Literature, James holds degrees from Northwestern and The University of St. Thomas. He resides in the Twin Cities and is a former board member for Graywolf Press.

Jenn Jones Sutliff is a Missouri native and writer currently living in Southern California. Her work has been published by *Pencil Box Press* and *Waxing and Waning Literary Journal*, among others.

Brandon Taylor is the author of the novels *The Late Americans* and *Real Life*, which was shortlisted for the Booker and National Book Critics Circle John Leonard Prize, and named a *New York Times Book Review* Editors' Choice, among others. His collection *Filthy Animals*, a national bestseller, was awarded The Story Prize and shortlisted for the Dylan Thomas Prize.

Abigail Thomas has twelve grandchildren, one great-grandchild, and two dogs. She lives in Woodstock, New York, and writes mostly memoir.

Michaella Thornton's writing often explores levity, lust, and letting go. Her work has appeared in *Brevity, Essay Daily, Fractured Lit, HAD, New South, Reckon Review, Southeast Review*, and The New Territory Magazine. Her prose has been nominated for Best of the Net, the Pushcart Prize, and Best Microfiction.

Allison K Williams is the author of *Seven Drafts: Self-Edit Like a Pro from Blank Page to Book*, and leads the Rebirth Your Book writing retreats series. A former aerialist and fire-eater, she lives in Dubai. Find her at allisonkwilliams.com.

Vonetta Young is a writer and strategy consultant based in Washington, D.C. Her essays and fiction have appeared in *Indiana Review*, *Barrelhouse*, *Lunch Ticket*, *Catapult*, and *Cosmonauts Avenue*, among others. She serves as Executive Editor at *The Offing*, as well as *Insight* (nonfiction) editor. She is twice a graduate of Georgetown University. Follow her on Instagram @VonettaWrites.

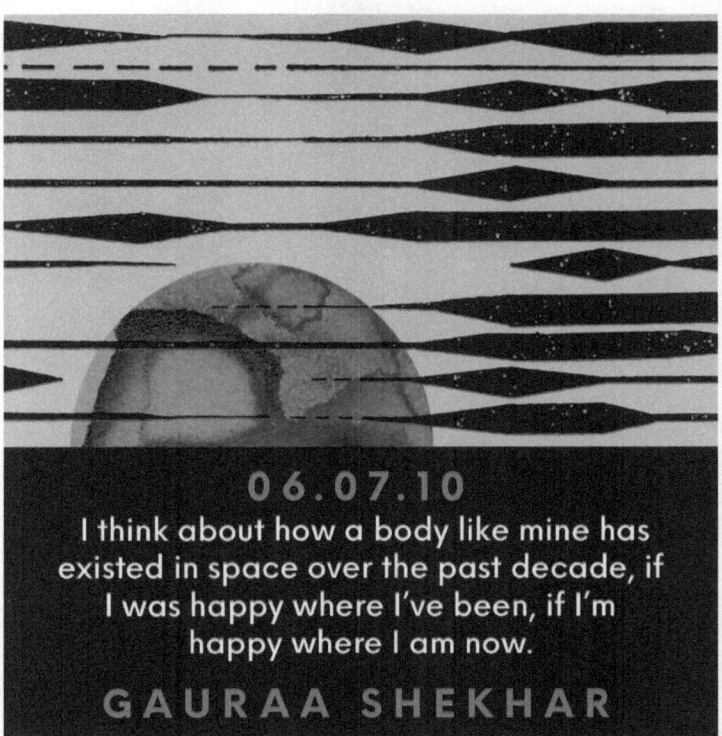

06.07.10
I think about how a body like mine has existed in space over the past decade, if I was happy where I've been, if I'm happy where I am now.

GAURAA SHEKHAR

ABOUT THE EDITORS

Dr. Donald E. Quist is author of two essay collections, *Harbors*, a Foreword INDIES Bronze Winner and International Book Awards Finalist, and *To Those Bounded*. He has a linked story collection, *For Other Ghosts*. His writing has appeared in *AGNI, North American Review, Michigan Quarterly Review, Poets & Writers, The Rumpus*, and was Notable in *Best American Essays 2018*. Donald has received fellowships from Sundress Academy for the Arts and Kimbilio Fiction. He is Assistant Professor of Creative Nonfiction at University of Missouri. Find him at donaldquist.com and @donaldewquist.

Kali White VanBaale is the author of the novels *The Monsters We Make, The Good Divide*, and *The Space Between*. She's the recipient of an American Book Award, an Eric Hoffer Book Award, and two State of Iowa major artist grants. Her short stories, essays, and articles have appeared in the A&E Network *True Crime* series, *The Coachella Review, The Chaffey Review, Nowhere Magazine, Poets & Writers*, and *The Writers' Chronicle*. Kali is a core faculty member of the Lindenwood University MFA Creative Writing Program, where she was named Adjunct Professor of the Year in 2022. Find her at kaliwhite.com and @kaliwriting.

Bailey Gaylin Moore is a PhD candidate studying Creative Writing at the University of Missouri–Columbia. Her debut essay collection, *Thank You for Staying with Me*, was published by University of Nebraska Press in 2025. Her writing has appeared in *AGNI, Pleiades, Wigleaf, Willow Springs*, and *Hayden's Ferry Review*. Find her at baileygaylinmoore.com and @baileygaylin.

ACKNOWLEDGMENTS

The editors of *The Past Ten* would like to give thanks to each and every contributor who has shared their story with us. We have been honored by the trust imparted to us in publishing these experiences online, and now in print. We have loved engaging with our artists/authors, it's been a gift in our lives.

None of this would be possible without our families—the VanBaales, the Whites, the Moores, the Palmers, and Quists—their love and support so often kept this project afloat. For all that you do, our beloveds, the ways you ground us and encourage our quirks and flourish, our *petit besoins*, we thank you. *Past Ten* is a testament to the enduring power of friendship, and this work owes its genesis to a conversation with a dear friend, Nicolas Leon Ruiz. It was nurtured by discussions with Colin Cheney. Our logo and launch were produced and guided by Panasit Ch. Ben Tanzer was crucial in expanding our contributors and reach. *Past Ten* would not exist without founding beliefs in *making* family through collaboration and art as an effective means of creating community.

The effort to bring a *Past Ten* anthology to fruition was aided by Marianne Merola, an early believer, and financial support from the Iowa Arts Council and the Authors Guild. Endless gratitude is owed to our publisher Dr. Ross K. Tangedal, Senior Editor Ellie Atkinson, Sales Director Sophie McPherson, Media Director Ava Willet, and the whole team at Cornerstone Press. We're so glad to have found such a great home for this project.

Lastly, we thank you dear reader, for taking time with these reflections. May they inspire you to keep going , keep living—through this to that.